EDUCATOR'S GUIDE TO
Immersion for Mission

FORMATION AND TRANSFORMATION THROUGH IMMERSION

Monica Dutton

VAUGHAN PUBLISHING

The *Educator's Guides*

The Mission and Education Project of BBI-TAITE (The Australian Institute of Theological Education) presents a series of Guides to serve the educational mission of Catholic schools in Australia and beyond. The Guides, each dealing with a specific area, introduce educators to ways in which mission and education may be integrated in the life and work of Catholic educators and students. The mandate given to the expert writers who create these Guides is to tap into the best available treatments of mission and also to ground their work in quality practice.

Therese D'Orsa
Professor Mission and Culture
BBI-TAITE
Commissioning Editor Mission and Education Project

Published in Australia by Vaughan Publishing
32 Glenvale Crescent, Mulgrave VIC 3170
A joint imprint of Garratt Publishing and BBI – The Australian Institute of Theological Education.

Copyright © 2021 Monica Dutton

All rights reserved. Except as provided by Australian copyright law, no part of this publication may be reproduced in any manner without prior permission in writing from the publisher.

Cover design and typesetting by Guy Holt
Images supplied by author: pp i, 1, 2, 3, 5, 9, 10, 11, 13, 14, 19, 20, 22, 24, 25, 26, 27, 28, 30, 38, 39, 43, 53, 54, 58 & cover
All other images supplied by iStock

The author and publisher gratefully acknowledge the permission granted to reproduce the copyright material in this book.
Every effort has been made to trace copyright holders and to obtain their permission for the use of copyright material.

The publisher apologises for any errors or omissions in the above list and would be grateful if notified of any corrections that should be incorporated in future reprints or editions of this book.

ISBN 9780648524632

 A catalogue record for this book is available from the National Library of Australia

Nihil Obstat: Reverend Gerard Diamond MA (Oxon), LSS, D. Theol
 Diocesan Censor
Imprimatur: Very Reverend Joseph Caddy AM Lic.Soc.Sci VG
 Vicar General
 Archdiocese of MelbourneDate: 10 November 2020

The *Nihil Obstat* and *Imprimatur* are official declarations that a book or pamphlet is free of doctrinal or moral error. No implication is contained therein that those who have granted the Nihil Obstat and Imprimatur agree with the contents, opinions or statements expressed. They do not necessarily signify that the work is approved as a basic text for catechetical instruction.

Dr Monica Dutton's *Educator's Guide to Immersion for Mission: Formation and Transformation through Immersion*, offers a valuable educational policy and curricular document, which synthesises globalisation, values and the Catholic tradition. It describes cross-cultural experiences through participants' engagement with other cultures and resultant transformational change in wisdom, knowledge, skills and values. The guide provides a pragmatic curriculum design for immersion programs, which intentionally situate participants in a cross-cultural setting. This guide is a superb, compelling and important text for educators, diocesan system leaders, religious institutes, school leadership and policy makers.

Associate Professor Joseph Zajda,
Australian Catholic University (Melbourne)

Dr Monica Dutton has written a superb immersion guide, which draws on years of practical experience and sound research. A must-have for education leaders when considering immersion trips for their staff and students.

Dr Wendy Moran, Principal Evaluator,
Centre for Education, Statistics and Evaluation
(NSW Department of Education)

Having had the pleasure of sharing many immersion experiences with Monica, I am delighted to see her research, wisdom and insight come together in this very practical guide.

The benefits of careful theological grounding and practical planning are there to see. The transformative experience offered to those who form true partnerships through this process can only enable genuine relationships characterised by 'soft eyes and warm hearts'.

Meg Kahler SGS

Dr Monica Dutton's work is a valuable contribution at a time when there is such strong interest in immersion experiences. This work highlights their profoundly transformative potential and provides clear theoretical and practical frameworks for their fruitful implementation. I recommend it as a guide to avoiding the many pitfalls faced by organisers ensuring that these experiences are mutually enriching to guest and host alike.

Dr Paul Lentern, Assistant Principal – Dean of Mission,
Mount St Benedict College, Pennant Hills

Born from lived experience and deep reflection on that experience, this guide offers new participants venturing into the privilege of immersion a practical, thought-provoking and interactional entry into what for many will be a transformational encounter with a Majority World community.

Moira Najdecki, Chair, Good Samaritan Education

An immersion experience is primarily about encountering and walking with the other, particularly the other whose culture, language and way of seeing the world is less familiar. An immersion experience can be challenging and even confronting but it remains a gift without measure, facilitating new friendships, new understandings and a growing sense of mutuality and respect. Dr Monica Dutton has provided a rich resource for anyone who seeks a deeper understanding of the place of immersion experiences to 'awaken and enliven' the spirit, allowing participants to meet the Christ who 'plays in ten thousand places, lovely in limbs, and lovely in eyes not his' ('As Kingfishers Catch Fire', G. M. Hopkins). Even more, this volume is also a practical and user-friendly guide for anyone planning an immersion. Monica's long and deep experience as an educator and immersion leader is evident in her thoughtful and detailed suggestions for structuring, planning and leading an immersion event.

Catherine Slattery SGS, Good Samaritan Education

An immersion has the potential to be an encounter of the heart for mind and spirit, thus for genuine personal transformation. Immersion for Mission is the fruit of obvious first-hand experience and offers practical, thorough, wise and sensitive advice for each stage of the immersion process and every contingency that may emerge. For educators wishing to engage in short-term cross-cultural immersion experiences, this book is certain to become the 'go-to' guide.

Patty Fawkner SGS, Congregational Leader,
Sisters of the Good Samaritan

Monica Dutton is an experienced educator, working with both youth and adults in the area of ministry and immersion experiences over many years. Monica's recent study and research underpin a deep understanding of the importance of immersion experiences and the impact of immersion on the communities with which they connect. The immersion experiences my staff have participated in with Monica's guidance have been transformative.

Elizabeth Carnegie, Principal,
Stella Maris College, Manly

To participate in an immersion is a privilege. It gives the participant opportunities and experiences that are long lasting and life changing. These guidelines provide a framework though which the immersion experience will be authentic, transformative and an expression of mission. Dr Monica Dutton has created a guide that illuminates the soul of immersion and provides the structures to enable participants to experience this soul.

Sue Lennox, Principal,
St Patrick's College, Campbelltown

Immersion experiences are often an awakening to new perspectives and new ways to see and live the Gospel. By their very nature, they challenge participants to step outside of their ordinary living. I commend this book to you as a practical guide on the planning and conduct of immersion experiences, to ensure it is a rich experience and one that delivers on the promise of transformation.

Dr Jane Comensoli, Executive Director,
Good Samaritan Education

Immersion experiences are invaluable learning opportunities that provide authentic encounters and build the participants' capacity to see the world from different perspectives. Such experiences require thoughtful preparation and clear methodology to ensure that they have long-term transformational effects for all involved. This evidence-based guide is a much-needed resource for educators and leaders that is highly accessible and practical in supporting the design of immersion experiences.

Christina He, Leader of Co-curricular,
Mount St Benedict College

Having had the privilege of being led by Dr Monica Dutton on immersion in the Philippines, I have experienced first-hand the deep spiritual impact of 'entering someone else's garden' with reverence, listening with humility and openness to change. Immersions infused with this mindset and theology result in ongoing partnerships, genuine relationships and a profound understanding of the Gospel.

Carolyn Collins, Head of Community & Social Justice,
Stella Maris College, Manly

This Educator's Guide lays out a three-phase immersion structure that ensures that one enters the experience well-informed, is able to sensitively experience the immersion and take quality time post-immersion to reflect and consider what to do next. Having attended numerous immersions organised and led by Dr Monica Dutton, I can attest to the experience from the very start of planning to the end-debrief and beyond. Immersion, as Dr Dutton states, 'cannot be entered into lightly'. It is truly a transforming experience that requires considered preparation and extensive follow-up afterwards.

This resource helps ensure that immersion experiences remain grounded in Gospel values and provide opportunities for meaningful dialogue and relationship-building with communities.

Kristie Ferguson,
Head of Year 12 & Teacher of Religious Education,
Stella Maris College, Manly

This is an excellent resource for supporting the design, planning and implementation of high-quality immersion experiences for adults and students. Monica has drawn on years of experience, knowledge and insights to share her wisdom in a practical guide that is deeply rooted in foundational principles of formation and Catholic Social Teaching. If you currently lead immersions or are considering future immersion programs I strongly recommend this book to you.

Mark Smith, Catholic Educator

It is obvious that this book has been written by someone with extensive knowledge in planning and facilitating immersions, but more importantly by one whose heart has been transformed by the experience. This is a go-to book that will assist leaders to prepare, coordinate and form their participants in such a way that the immersion experience will nourish the head, heart and hands. For me, this book connects the dots and ensures that immersions are done for the right reason, that participants are prepared well and that there is a real and authentic connection in bringing about the kingdom.

Donna Dempsey, Leader of Religious Education,
Mission and Formation.

Contents

Foreword		2
Introduction		3
Chapter 1	What is immersion?	5
Chapter 2	Planning an immersion	9
Chapter 3	Pre-immersion phase	20
Chapter 4	Immersion phase	23
Chapter 5	Post-immersion phase	33
Chapter 6	Immersion and formation	40
Chapter 7	Immersion and transformation	44
Chapter 8	Theological reflection for mission	46
Chapter 9	Soft eyes, warm heart	52
Chapter 10	Conclusion	56
Helpful terms		57
Endnotes		58
Suggested further reading		59
Acknowledgments		60

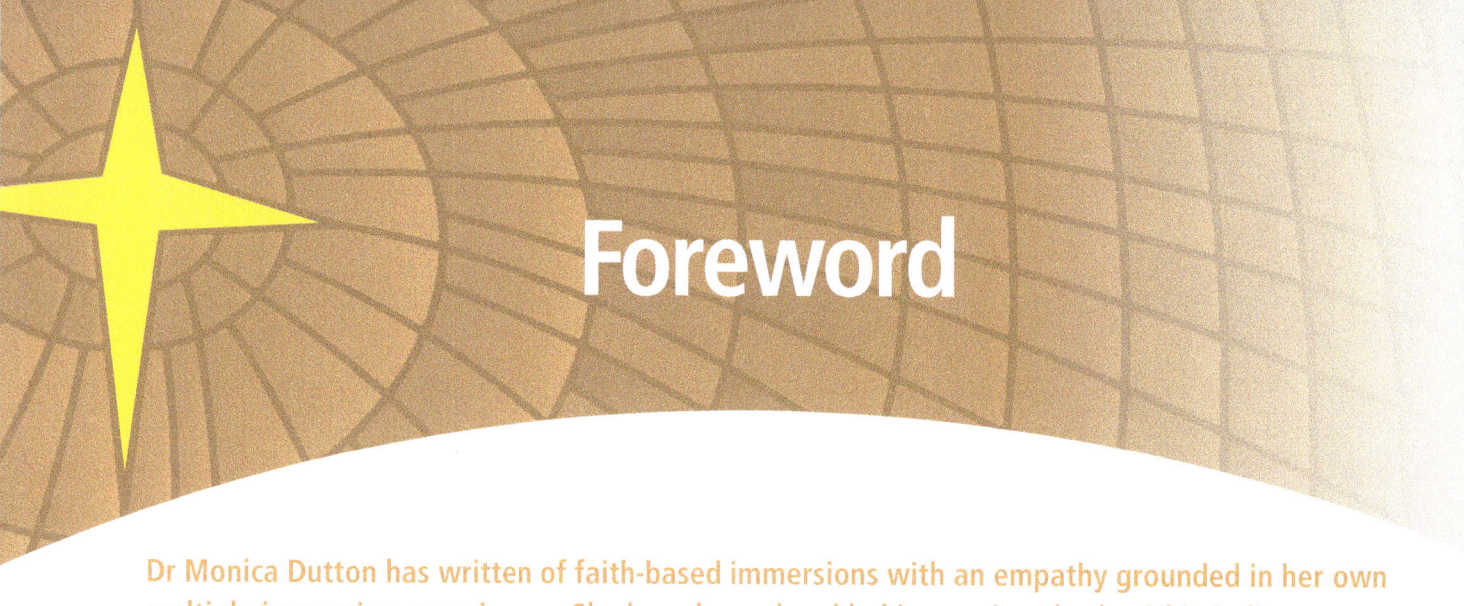

Foreword

Dr Monica Dutton has written of faith-based immersions with an empathy grounded in her own multiple immersion experiences. She has planned and led immersions both within indigenous communities in Australia and in several countries in Southeast Asia over more than 15 years.

More importantly, in writing a guide for those planning immersions, Dr Dutton has engaged with the social, personal, cultural and theological components of an immersion, providing helpful reflection points along the way.

This text has grown out of Dr Dutton's doctoral work where she reflected upon numerous immersions encountered by schools in the Good Samaritan tradition. The deep caring of this tradition clearly shines from these pages and centres immersion as an experience of the heart rather than of travel.

I value Monica's chapters on 'post-immersion' as an acknowledgment that the work of immersion is not completed upon return to one's home country. Monica's chapters on theological reflection emphasise that this work of the heart is such that host communities are frequently those that offer most to the experience, and immersion participants are the recipients of this gift.

This guide is a 'must have' for leaders and indeed participants of immersions. Not only should leaders have this guide, I recommend it as a planning tool for each community anticipating offering immersion experiences.

Dr Roger Vallance, FMS

Introduction

This is the wallpaper on my iPhone – has been for many years now. I keep it because it is a reminder of something else, something much more important than an iPhone…

The colourful, shambolic disarray indicates the excited rush of little ones eager to get inside. They need to take off their shoes before entering the house – and do so in such a hurry that their sandals and thongs end up strewn about in a chaotic rainbow heap.

The children are looking forward to joining a Scripture class in the Boulevard, a squatter settlement just outside Bacolod in the Philippines. There they gather each week for songs, prayers, scripture readings, a small treat and the love the Sisters of the Good Samaritan have for each and every one of them. To witness this joyous, colourful cacophony through an immersion experience is to be changed forever.

Immersions are an authentic encounter and engagement with another culture, which can be at the same time uncomfortable, confronting and challenging. Many participants speak of a 'moment' during their immersion, or a 'light-bulb' experience, which causes a fundamental shift in their outlook. If they are open to being changed by that moment, it is not possible to go back to the way they were before, and they can never see the world in quite the same way again. It causes them to reposition themselves in the world.

The transformative effect of immersion trips has been well documented. It is an encounter of the heart, the mind and the spirit, and provides an opportunity for participants to step back, refocus, and reassess their priorities. Immersion offers a counterpoint for how individuals view the world and their own place in it.

Authentic immersion experiences are deeply relational. They involve real people, real communities and real stories. They are about understanding and experiencing first-hand what life is like for another person. They are about listening and learning. Immersions are not

so much about walking in someone else's shoes; but rather about walking with, or walking beside, the other. Immersion experiences are about coming to know someone else's story, and then becoming a part of each other's story.

As well as an attitudinal shift, immersion experiences can awaken and enliven the spirit. Involvement in the richness and diversity of the Catholic tradition in another cultural setting provides a global picture of Church. Witnessing the ministries and compassion of those who work in culturally diverse communities on a daily basis is to come to know Christ in a 21st century context.

Immersion experiences can also provide a way to reconnect with personal spirituality through participation in a liberating expression of faith and life. There are times of stillness, reflection and peace which invite the presence of God. There is also a restorative dimension – a sense of hope, joy and peace; and often a recognition of, and a reawakening to, something we have lost in the hi-tech whirlwind of our daily existence. Immersion experiences provide an opportunity for people to pause, to take stock and to re-evaluate. By their very nature they are confronting. Participants are commonly quite unsettled after returning home, until they are able to make some sense of their experience and what it means for their lives.

In the long-term many speak of reconnecting to their immersion experience in later years to inform decisions made in their personal and professional lives. They have been humbled by the privilege of the immersion encounter, and afterwards feel impelled to somehow make a difference in their own time and place. There are often intentional and purposeful reminders of the immersion in their daily lives and actions, which can take them back to the experience in a heartbeat.

My iPhone wallpaper is one such reminder. It tells a story – I have no intention of changing it. It takes me back to an experience of encounter and engagement, of learning and living differently, and ultimately of transformation. It is part of my story, part of who I am. It keeps me grounded.[1]

This guide provides a unique insight into the multi-faceted, complex experience of immersion. Personal experiences and practical examples offer a singular lens through which to view immersion in the context of mission, while at the same time providing a useful guide to planning and facilitation of trips. This guide is intended for use by diocesan system leaders, religious institutes, ministerial public juridic persons, school leadership teams, mission leaders, social justice coordinators, parishes and all those involved in building and strengthening partnerships with rural, remote, Indigenous and Majority World communities.

It is hoped this guide will provide a valuable resource for those wishing to undertake the process of leading others through an experience of personal encounter and cross-cultural engagement, with the ultimate aim of enlivening God's mission in the world today.

CHAPTER 1

What is immersion?

Immersion experiences are a relatively new phenomenon. There has been a sharp rise in interest and involvement in these experiences, particularly in the Australian educational context. Factors contributing to this include more affordable travel, greater accessibility to host communities, increased awareness of global issues and a desire to be personally involved in action, advocacy, and solidarity with those in the Majority World.

Immersions have been variously described and defined. In general terms, learning experiences outside the usual environment are referred to as 'field trips' or 'study tours'. In some circles, when the experience includes a cross-cultural or service component, the term used is 'immersion trip' or 'exposure trip'. In the United States, such experiences are referred to as 'mission trips'. Generally speaking, an immersion refers to a period of time during which participants, usually from the developed world, visit and engage with people in a cross-cultural setting in a Majority World community.

Short-term cross-cultural immersion experiences typically involve leaving one's own community for a short period of time, with the majority of trips lasting around two weeks. The aims of immersions vary greatly and may include evangelism, service provision, cultural immersion, education and social justice advocacy. Motivations of participants may include desiring to have a challenging or meaningful experience, hoping to make a difference by helping others, or wishing to gain greater cross-cultural understanding. Benefits for host communities include increased understanding of global thought and concepts, development of supportive partnerships and access to financial and practical assistance.

Globalisation and the articulated outcomes of higher education such as the acquisition of intercultural knowledge, competence and engagement, have seen the inclusion of international studies, and exchange and immersion programs in many schools and universities. At the same time, immersion trips have been found to inspire participants to challenge and transform their previously held cross-cultural beliefs and understandings.

Typically, participants describe their immersion experience 'life-changing', 'transformative' or a 'light-bulb moment'. In many cases the trips appear to spark greater awareness of global inequity, which then becomes a catalyst for personal involvement in action and advocacy in the post-immersion phase. Participants commonly describe feeling both humbled and enriched by their experience, and actively seek out ways to 'give back' after returning home.

The concept of transformation through immersion has been identified and described as "entering into a foreign medium in the form of a culture or sub-culture and consequently emerging [as] a changed person"[2]. Importantly, an immersion needs to be an experience of solidarity with the local people and cannot be experienced without personal engagement and reflection.

Immersion experiences are characterised not only by visits to host communities, but by "conversation with local people, identification of concerns, exposure to and exploration of traditional cultures and their values, and analysis of global influences and current social issues"[3].

The upsurge in frequency of immersions in recent years has generated a remarkable diversity of destinations and anticipated outcomes for both participants and for organising entities. Corporate and not-for-profit organisations including humanitarian, secular and faith-based groups all expend a great deal of time, energy and resources on planning and facilitating immersion trips.

The 21st century has seen a rapid expansion in the popularity of immersions in a range of settings. In response to the growth in the popularity of immersion experiences, this guide aims to explore short-term cross-cultural immersion experiences within the context of giving life and expression to God's mission.

Immersion for mission

Formation is central to the life and mission of Catholic schools. Its purpose is deep learning through a range of intentional, ongoing and reflective experiences, leading to the transformation of individuals and educational communities. While cross-cultural immersions are still relatively new, their popularity has increased exponentially in recent times, and they are becoming widely recognised as a way of inviting staff, students and those in governance positions into an authentic and life-giving "kingdom space". As immersion for mission is a vehicle for Catholic education, the design and development of programs need to be embedded in the Gospel message, and the spirituality at the heart of the Catholic tradition.

Stated aims of Australian Catholic schools include encouraging students to develop an international perspective on their own country, and to discover how their country can identify and respond justly to its international obligations. Catholic schools therefore strive to prioritise events involving active community service, and issues of social justice informed by Catholic Social Teaching. *The Framework for Formation for Mission in Catholic Education*[4] highlights the importance of developing capabilities for mission and service in the Church and the world. If these aims are to be met with authenticity and integrity, it is critical that members of Catholic school communities be provided with engaging, experiential and developmental opportunities which include a cross-cultural dimension.

Schools that articulate their expression of Catholicism through a particular charism have also revitalised their emphasis on programs to facilitate this approach and offer immersion and pilgrimage opportunities for members of their school communities. Participants engage with the charism by connecting to the history, traditions, spirituality, and contemporary expression of its mission, with a particular focus on ministries involved with vulnerable and marginalised people.

The starting point for developing social justice programs aimed at individual and spiritual growth is to make them personally meaningful. Designing immersion programs which intentionally situate participants in cross-cultural settings leads to direct encounters and engagement with communities at risk. Engaging with the heart of the Gospel message through holistic concern for others as a result of an immersion experience, opens the possibility for individual and communal transformation.

Catholic immersions are Christocentric, promote a Catholic worldview, aim to deepen an awareness and appreciation of the Catholic tradition in another cultural context, and involve participants in experiences that invite a response from the heart, soul, strength and mind. Catholic immersion experiences are underpinned by a Catholic anthropology, contemporary theologies and the principles of Catholic Social Teaching, thereby providing opportunities for action and advocacy that resonate strongly with staff, students and parents.

Along with contemplative and reflective practices, the embodiment of the Gospel message in the Catholic tradition is found in outreach and service to others. This transformational vision at the heart of the Gospel couples with the social justice imperative of the Catholic school. With Jesus as model, immersions link participants to contemporary Catholic ministries through themes of partnership, service and spirituality. Through personal engagement with God's mission in the world today, it becomes clear to participants that Catholic social justice is not optional, and not peripheral to the Gospel invitation.

All of these aspects point to the philosophical and theological underpinnings of short-term cross-cultural immersion. As such, the selection of this increasingly popular experience in the Catholic school setting is well founded.

Immersions have been described as being nothing less than building the Kingdom of God.

Aidan Donaldson
(Irish writer, lecturer, social justice activist)

The key principles that underpin immersion for mission.

Immersion for mission:

- is framed within the Catholic context
- is authentically grounded in the Gospel message
- is informed by Catholic Social Teaching, respecting the principles of human dignity, the common good, solidarity and subsidiarity
- advocates the principles of Liberation Theology, particularly in relation to the preferential option for the poor
- is informed by contemporary approaches to mission, theology and cross-cultural engagement
- provides compassion, a listening ear, and a voice for those facing issues of injustice
- encompasses formation and deep learning through experiential and transformative learning processes
- is a prayerful, spiritual and reflective experience
- engages a spirit of dialogue and partnership with host communities
- provides opportunities for encounters with difference
- promotes transformative outcomes in terms of internal shift and changed perspectives and behaviours
- involves three distinct phases (pre-immersion, immersion and post-immersion)
- prioritises the building of mutually beneficial relationships
- engages in respectful dialogue
- seeks to empower and support host communities
- enlivens the spirit and awakens possibilities for mission
- respects the environment of the host community and the need to conserve precious resources

Immersion for mission does not:

- create unhealthy dependencies or 'hand-out' mentalities
- engage in voyeurism, 'voluntourism' or poverty tourism
- deplete fragile resources in the host community

Figure 1. Guiding principles for immersion for mission

Think about, talk about…

1. What three aspects of immersion for mission do you consider to be the most important?
2. Which of these aspects are clearly evident in your planning for immersion?
3. What are some practical examples of these aspects from your own experiences of immersion?

CHAPTER 2
Planning an immersion

An immersion experience cannot be entered into lightly. A number of critical factors need to be taken into consideration when contemplating the possibility of taking a group of adults or students on a short-term cross-cultural immersion trip. Why, where, when, who, what and how you would undertake the planning, organisation and facilitation of an immersion must be carefully addressed at the outset.

The structure of immersion

Immersion needs to be understood as an ongoing process, which occurs across three interrelated and co-dependent phases. Each phase builds upon the previous one. Importantly, the timeframe for the impact of the experience is neither linear nor finite.

The three phases are:

- the pre-immersion phase
- the immersion experience itself
- the post-immersion phase

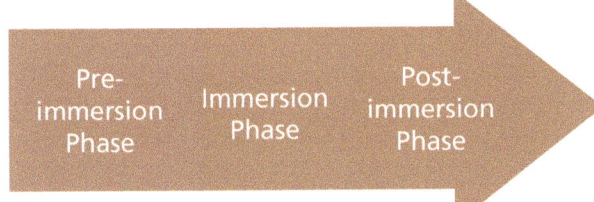

Figure 2. Three phases of the immersion process

Given the particular nature of immersion, participation in all three phases is critical. An immersion trip experienced in isolation is meaningless. It is also important to note that organising entities have significant responsibilities to participants and to the host community in all three phases. Each of the phases of immersion is explored in depth throughout the following chapters.

Planning Phase

The planning process for an immersion may be approached by asking a sequence of interrelated questions, each one informing the context of the next. First and foremost, organisers need to be very clear about precisely *why* they would take a group on an immersion trip. What is the rationale for the immersion? What are you hoping to achieve? Prayerful reflection leading to discernment and clarity of purpose is crucial to this process.

Distilling the *why* of your immersion informs the second most important factor, the *where*. With these elements in place, consideration can then be given to the *when* and the *who*, and finally, the *what* and the *how*. It is imperative to have transparency around these aspects before planning begins. The sequence of reflection is outlined in Figure 3 and detailed in the following sections.

Why are you going?

Discerning precisely why you might undertake to organise an immersion is the first and most important step. It informs your approach to planning, and everything else flows from there. The following questions may assist in guiding and developing your thinking.

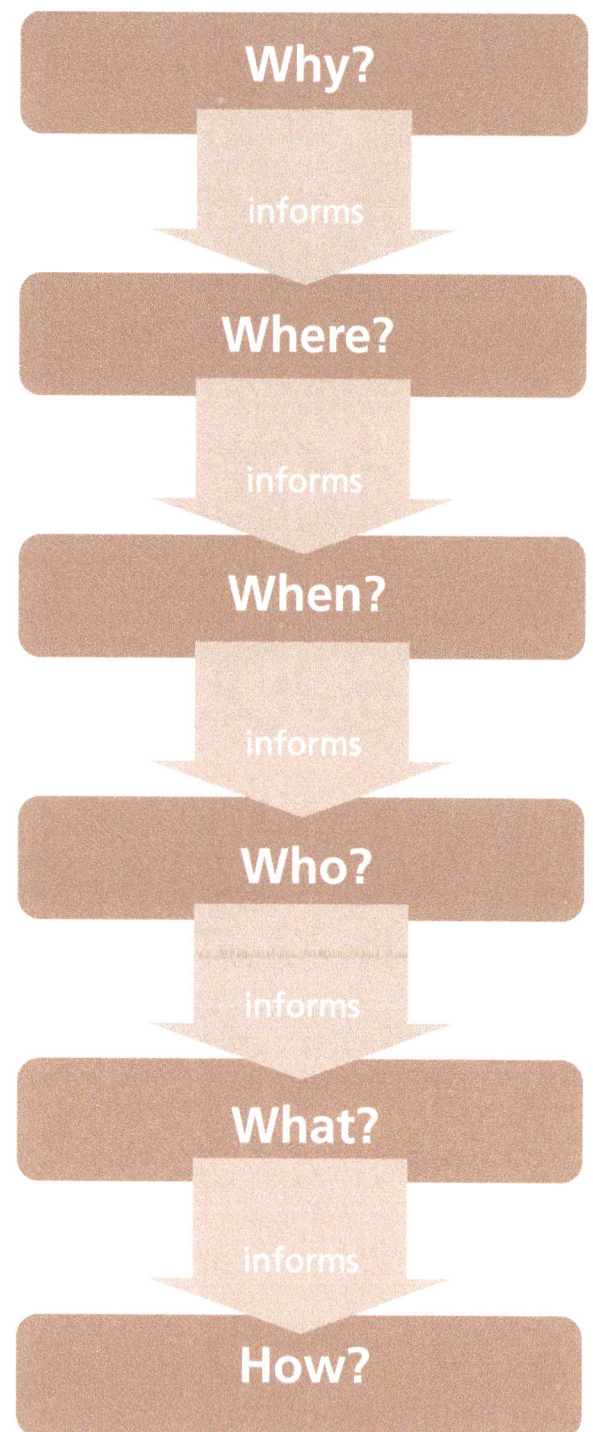

Figure 3. Reflection process before planning an immersion

- What is the rationale for the immersion?
- What is the Gospel focus?
- What are the theological underpinnings?
- What does the Church tell us about this?
- What aspects of Catholic Social Teaching are emphasised?
- What understanding of mission and missionary discipleship will inform the planning?
- Is there a call to conversion? To action?
- What are the opportunities for formation and transformation?
- What are the anticipated outcomes?

Figure 4. Perspectives for consideration in planning an immersion

Where will you go?

The most important consideration in determining the location for an immersion is the relationship with the host community. A slow and intentional building of long-term partnerships between schools, dioceses and host communities is essential and 'one-off' or 'fly-in, fly-out' models are to be avoided at all cost. Dialogue, mutual respect and a common understanding of

Questions for consideration

First, ask yourself:

- Why am I thinking of planning an immersion?
- What am I hoping to achieve?

When you are able to discern the essence of these two questions, it is essential to take some time for prayerful reflection in considering different perspectives for your immersion before you begin to plan.

Think about, talk about…

1. What aspects of the Catholic tradition best inform your approach to planning an immersion experience?
2. How is God's mission being enlivened and sustained through your approach to immersion?
3. How might the words and actions of Jesus be made known to participants and the host community through your planning?
4. How is justice being proclaimed and witnessed through your approach to immersion?

purpose are key to these relationships. Religious institutes, ministerial public juridic persons, diocesan systems, and a number of Catholic agencies such as Caritas and Catholic Mission already have well established links to communities in rural, remote, indigenous and Majority World communities. Supporting and working within these established frameworks is always a good place to start. The important thing is to ensure the relationship with the community is respectful and has the potential to develop into a life-giving, long-term partnership.

Accessibility and infrastructure within the host community are also important considerations. Travelling on public transport with local operators can provide a real sense of life in another culture and can be a good way to engage with people in the community. It is worth thoroughly checking available options though, as duty of care is paramount and risk management strategies need to be carefully addressed.

When choosing accommodation, it is extremely important to be aware of the fragile nature of some host communities, and to focus on not depleting precious resources such as food, water and energy. While homestay may appear to provide a more 'authentic' experience, host communities often go above and beyond their means in accommodating guests. If possible, it is often better to opt for independent accommodation in local hostels and purchasing meals from nearby food outlets. This also provides a respectful way of contributing to the economy while engaging with the community through a range of planned and incidental activities. Visiting homes in the host community should always be at the invitation of the local people and not an expectation of visitors.

Availability and reliability of communication networks and devices, and access to medical and consular assistance, also need to be considered. As some communities are quite remote, knowledge and action plans for accessing medical help, should it be required,

Think about, talk about...

1. Considerations around practicality and cost are important in determining the 'where' of the immersion.
2. Is the location of the community practical in the timeframe available for the trip?
3. Is the location manageable for the capacity of the particular group travelling?
4. Is the cost prohibitive?
5. Would the money spent on getting there be more useful to the community if spent in some other way?
6. Is it better to partner with this community in some other way?
7. Would it be better to partner with a different community?

need to be clearly in place before arriving. Similarly, it is always wise to register travel plans and contact details with the local Australian embassy, consulate or high commission.

When will you go?

The timing and duration of an immersion trip is entirely dependent on dialogue between the host community and the immersion organisers. While school groups tend to prefer the extended periods of time afforded by term-breaks, this would need to be negotiated and is dependent on a range of factors affecting the host community.

Awareness of seasonal weather patterns, health risks, cultural events, religious festivals and the political climate are all essential considerations. Seasonal weather patterns, particularly in the region of Southeast Asia, can be very unpredictable. It is advisable to avoid travelling in the monsoon season. Along with possible interruptions to travel plans, your presence during the monsoon season may place additional burdens on the local people if they need to try to feed and accommodate stranded visitors while addressing their own issues of homelessness, cleaning-up, rebuilding, and accessing adequate food and a clean water supply. In these situations, a Plan B is always essential!

While participation in cultural events and religious festivals is a wonderful way to experience life in a different context, again, care needs to be taken so as not to overburden the local people. Fasting and feasting are part of the rhythm of life in cross-cultural communities, and it is important to ensure participation of visitors does not cause additional pressure. It is also worthwhile to consider that calendared events in the local community such as school holidays or exams may also preclude the involvement of students in planned activities at certain times. School visits and interaction with students are wonderful ways to engage participants in the life and culture of the local community, and a mutually beneficial way to learn and practise each other's language skills.

Awareness of the political climate in the country and community visited is also a critical factor. Is there an upcoming election? Have skirmishes been reported?

Think about, talk about...

1. What particular factors would need to be taken into consideration when determining the most suitable time to visit the host community you are in partnership with?

It is also important to ensure your presence does not contribute to a situation that is already potentially volatile. It is wise to avoid all public gatherings and rallies, not to wear or carry any politically motivated slogans or symbols, and to always abide by the directions of the local authorities. Familiarity with advice provided by the Australian Department of Foreign Affairs and Trade (DFAT) during the planning stage is essential.

Awareness of updates provided by the Australian Government's *Smartraveller* website will also alert immersion organisers to health risks prevalent at different times of the year in different regions, along with recommended vaccinations and precautions.

Who will go?

While many people express a desire to go on an immersion trip, those who put themselves forward usually have a genuine interest and possess a certain predisposition for the experience. They are often in search of something 'more' in life, and an immersion experience provides an avenue for them to further explore that desire in a very practical way.

Expressing an interest in going on an immersion, however, is not sufficient reason for inclusion in the group. The situation where involvement in an immersion experience is the desire of the parents rather than the student, would also need to be approached with caution. The criteria for selection of participants need to clearly address the purpose, expectations and anticipated outcomes of the experience. Possible considerations may include that a person:

- displays a capacity to make a positive contribution to a group
- is generous and community minded
- has a keen interest in issues of justice
- displays a capacity for service to others
- responds positively to opportunities for prayer and reflection
- has an open mind and an open heart
- is capable of clearly articulating ideas, thoughts and feelings
- is a positive influence within the school community
- understands the Catholic view of mission and missionary discipleship

Through interviews, focus groups and written reflections, applicants would be of concern if they emerge as being judgemental; have a 'saviour complex'; demonstrate overly privileged perspectives; or have the belief that they can solve the complex, multi-layered and multi-faceted issues of injustice and poverty in the host community. In any of these scenarios, their capacity to engage meaningfully with the local people, and to contribute positively to the group they travel with, would be questionable at best.

School visits and interaction with students are wonderful ways to engage participants in the life and culture of the local community...

The overriding motivation for many people going on an immersion trip is to 'do' something or to 'help' the people they are visiting. While this approach may be well-intentioned, invariably people in host communities want to talk, to be listened to, to be heard. They want their stories to be told. Although a service component may be highly valuable, participant actions must be guided and moderated by the needs of the host community.

It is also important to consider the impact the size of a group can have on the host community. As mentioned previously, depletion of resources in the host community is a critical consideration. Physically managing a large group may also provide challenges for organisers and for the community. Additionally, in cases where there are large numbers in the visiting group, there is a tendency for them to stay together, rather than step out of their comfort zone and talk to people in the host community. This results in not engaging as meaningfully with the local people, thus diminishing opportunities for both developing a relationship with the host community, and personal transformation.

It is critical that group leaders are well chosen, and ideally there should be a minimum of two. This way if an issue arises, one can manage the situation, while the other continues with the group program. The role of a leader is diverse, demanding and by no means limited to that of a tour guide. As familiarity with the local context is necessary on a daily basis, it is essential that at least one of the leaders has visited the host community previously. Many organisations operate on a rotating system whereby a person goes as an assistant leader one year and then leads the trip the following year, taking another assistant along with them. Good communication and rapport between leaders, and clarity around role descriptions, are essential.

A low-stress approach and skills in managing group dynamics are also important characteristics of group leaders. Along with tiredness, illness and homesickness, being in an unfamiliar environment and culture can have a very unsettling effect on some participants. Being flexible and attentive to the needs of the group can mitigate the impact of possible tensions or conflict.

Think about, talk about…

1. What knowledge, experience and skills do you believe immersion group leaders need to possess?
2. What do you believe to be the most important criteria to consider in the process of selecting participants?
3. How would you go about planning the selection process for participants in your school/organisation? What would you need to take into account?

What will you do?

As with all aspects of an immersion, planning the itinerary needs to be negotiated with people in the host community. The key to organisation is flexibility. It is often better to have an overall plan with room for movement, rather than a more structured approach which is timed to the last minute. Host communities generally tend to operate on a much less rigid approach to time than Western cultures, so it is often best to just 'go with the flow'.

In order to provide participants with an understanding of what life is like for the people in the host community, it is important to include visits to sites of historical, geographical, cultural, political and religious significance. Engagement with the local people through involvement in cultural and religious celebrations is a particularly good way to come to an understanding of the interpersonal and intergenerational way of life typical in many Majority World communities. Visits to educational, health care, welfare and community agencies also highlight the opportunities and challenges faced by people in the host country on a daily basis.

Building relationships with people in the local community and listening to their stories is central to the purpose of all immersions, and should be the priority when planning the itinerary. Learning local arts, crafts, songs and dances, along with cooking, playing sport and visiting markets, provides wonderful firsthand insights into life for the local people.

The inclusion of a service component must always and only be through dialogue with the host community, and even then only after mutual trust and respect have been established. The needs articulated by the local people must be prioritised over needs perceived by participants, and their preferred activities. Teaching classes for example, may be enjoyable for participants, but not necessarily useful or helpful for the schools. Involvement in building projects is also often well beyond the experience and capacity of participants, and at the expense of employing local people to monitor or supervise the work. Building walls should never replace building relationships.

> *We are called to be with people, patiently waiting to discern with them what the Spirit is calling us all to. Our lives should be characterised by attentiveness, graciousness, humility and contemplation rather than frenetic activity.*
>
> Noel Connolly SSC

Similarly, donations must only be considered in consultation with the host community. It is often better to contribute to the local economy by spending money in shops and markets rather than bringing donations from home. Donations of school supplies and text

Think about, talk about…

1. What are the most effective ways for your group to engage with the host community?
2. How might these activities contribute to deepening the partnership with the host community?

books are not always useful as they commonly don't align with the requirements of the local curriculum. Even well-intentioned donations such as items of clothing may inadvertently destroy fragile cottage industries such as sewing, which have been established through micro-finance agencies. The key factor in all aspects of the relationship is dialogue.

It is also essential to provide a balanced, well-paced program for participants. A first visit to a Majority World community can be overwhelming, as well as physically, mentally and emotionally draining. It is therefore important to factor in opportunities for adequate personal time, rest and relaxation, and reflection and debriefing.

How will you do it?

Conducting an immersion experience requires meticulous planning and attention to detail. While a degree of flexibility is required, nothing should be left to chance, and in every situation a 'Plan B' always needs to have been considered.

In the planning phase, it is essential to do your homework. Use reputable travel companies and operators, and check the locality and safety of accommodation options. While all travel involves an element of chance, when taking a school group on an immersion trip, carefully considered compliant risk management strategies need to be in place. Ask other schools and agencies who they deal with, and seek advice from your contact person in the host community. It is essential to ensure risk management plans are specific to the destination and to the particular members of the group, and that strategies are audited and updated regularly.

During the immersion, constant monitoring of the group, thorough pre-planning and briefing for each day's activities, assists in safeguarding the wellbeing of both the participants and the people in the host community. Anticipating unexpected issues and managing them as they arise helps to prevent potentially difficult situations from escalating. Keep asking yourself "what if …"

After the immersion it is important to consider how and when you will evaluate the experience. Feedback sheets, online surveys, individual interviews and focus group discussions may all provide helpful information for future planning. The timing of the evaluation is also an important consideration. In the immediate, post-immersion phase participants are often 'on a high' after their experience and are more inclined to provide overly positive responses.

In this case it may well be worth doing a follow-up evaluation six to 12 months later. This timeframe may also provide valuable information about whether the initial reaction to the experience has diminished or intensified over time, and whether changed perspectives as a result of the immersion have translated into plans for action.

Some organisations also utilise a pre- and post-immersion inventory in relation to determining changes in participant levels of knowledge, attitudes, skills and aspirations. Increased levels of empathy and compassion have also been tracked in pre- and post-immersion questionnaires.

In the planning phase, it is essential to do your homework...

In summary

		Factors to Consider
Why *are you going?*	Guiding principles	• rationale/context (e.g. partnership, service, spirituality) • Gospel focus • theological underpinnings • Church teaching including Catholic Social Teaching • understanding of mission and missionary discipleship • opportunities for formation and transformation • anticipated outcomes • is there a call to conversion, to action?
Where *will you go?*	Host community	• partnership • accessibility • transport and accommodation options • cost
When *will you go?*	Timing and duration	• seasonal weather patterns • cultural and religious events and festivals • school breaks at home and in the host community • political climate in the region
Who *will go?*	Leaders and participants	• experience of group leaders • selection criteria for participants
What *will you do?*	Itinerary	• inclusion of aspects relating to historical, geographical, cultural, political, religious, educational, and socio-economic perspectives • a well-balanced itinerary which includes opportunities for engagement with the local people, adequate personal time, and time for rest, relaxation and reflection • a service component and donations considered only in dialogue with the host community • involvement in prayer and liturgy
How *will you do it?*	Practicalities	• transport • accommodation • safety and wellbeing • risk management strategies

Figure 5. Helpful perspectives in planning an immersion

Why are you going?

Where will you go?

When will you go?

Who will go?

What will you do?

How will you do it?

Figure 6. Reflection template for immersion planning

It is also imperative to consider how you might obtain feedback from the host community and how you might develop ongoing plans for deepening the partnership. It would be of significant concern if the next time they hear from you is when you are wanting to plan another immersion trip!

Think about, talk about…

Using the information in this chapter and the summary table on page 17, complete an immersion planning reflection template (page 18) for your school, diocese, parish or organisation.

Think about, talk about…

1. What are the inherent risks of immersion experiences for participants?
2. What are the inherent risks for the host community?
3. How might you mitigate these risks in your planning?
4. What methods of evaluation might you use with your immersion group?
5. What methods of evaluation might you use with the host community?

CHAPTER 3
Pre-immersion phase

Pre-immersion is the phase during which organisation and preparation take place. Briefing sessions and preparation sessions for participants are crucial elements of this phase. Essentially, briefing sessions are concerned with providing information and preparation sessions involve opportunities for formation.

To ensure that participants understand and engage with the process, it is essential to provide clarity of purpose for the immersion and connections to unifying features of the group and the host community. Similarly, it is critical to contextualise the host community's historical, political, social, cultural and religious dimensions. Together, these aspects offer participants pathways to understanding and anchor points in the midst of potential uncertainty and disequilibrium while on the immersion.

Briefing Sessions

Briefing sessions encompass the practicalities of an immersion. Essentially, briefing is concerned with providing *information* – understanding the *where, when, who, what* and *how* of the immersion. Sessions may include aspects such as:

- contextualising the host community
  - history, geography, political and socio-economic factors, cultural and religious traditions, customs and language
- travel advice
  - vaccinations, medications, food and water, climate and weather conditions, luggage and packing (travelling lightly)
  - currency, electricity converters, access to communication
- personal safety and wellbeing
  - culture shock, group dynamics, local laws, personal health
- cultural sensitivities
  - culturally sensitive attire, minimising displays of wealth and privilege, living simply
  - seeking permission before photographing anyone or anything
  - respect and responsible use of social media
- documentation
  - passport, visa, insurance, medical forms, emergency contacts

Preparation Sessions

Preparation sessions, on the other hand, focus on *formation* – the *why* of the immersion. That is, providing participants with the opportunity to be able to fully engage in the immersion process, and to the possibility of being changed by the experience. Preparation sessions would include engagement with the questions that inform the conduct of your planned immersion.

One way to prepare for an immersion experience is to consider the metaphor of 'entering someone else's garden'. Roger Schroeder SVD[5] has worked in the area of cross-cultural mission, and has developed a helpful framework in relation to thinking about experiences of another culture. Much of Schroeder's work took place in Papua New Guinea where the garden is the food source of the community. He uses the metaphor that anytime we leave our own time and place, and enter into another culture, we *enter someone else's garden*. When we do this, there are four main questions to consider.

Why are you entering someone's garden?

Schroeder suggests the following starting point:

"One approaches the 'other' with the idea that God is already present. Underlying this approach is a radical trust and belief in the power of God's spirit at work in the lives and cultures of people – people who are different from oneself, who often may be poor and marginalised, who share one's fundamental human dignity, rights, and responsibilities, and who are one's sisters and brothers created in God's image".

How do you enter someone's garden for the first time?

Schroeder suggests we are strangers in another's garden, and we have many things to learn. If an immersion experience does not leave you with questions about how life is for others, then you need to do it again!

"I learned that good intentions are not enough and that mistakes are made when entering into someone else's world. I learned about their hospitality and patience with an 'outsider'. I made mistakes and that helped me to see what I had learned through it! Such a lesson should not leave the 'newcomer' paralysed with the fear of making further mistakes, but one is reminded both of one's child-like knowledge and status in the new culture and therefore the need to be an attentive learner."

What do you 'do' in someone's garden?

Schroeder is clear that we must remember two rules when we enter someone else's garden:

Rule 1: It is not ours and we should always have the good sense to know that we must work with people. How would you feel if someone walked into your garden and started criticising and pulling plants out without really taking the time to get to know why your garden is like it is!

"You are very welcome to work with us in the community, but remember that this is our community. We don't want you to come in with your solutions to our situation."

Rule 2: Our view is only one view. We can only see things from where we stand. The challenge is to be open to see the world from another stand point.

"We naturally tend to perceive, understand and judge someone else's 'world' through the 'lens' of our own."

What happens in your own garden?

If we truly enter someone else's garden, our own garden should change. We will be able to transplant, grow new things, and learn about other plants if we walk in another garden. The experience helps us to see new things. We can contribute to another's garden but we should also be open to having our garden change because of what we can learn from another.

"When life is seen as a conversation, it means that we become persons immersed in the world of others, like Jesus was in our world. It is with people, therefore, that we begin to ask questions; it is with people that basic human values are endorsed and challenged; and it is this context that shapes the way of announcing the Good News and of challenging structures that imprison people."

As people of different cultures share their expressions and experiences of the 'Good News', the possibility for a more authentic and complete image of Christianity emerges. As we move from our narrow path of understanding, we are challenged to participate more fully in God's mission of compassion, justice and love.

Think about, talk about…

1. Take some time to reflect upon the four questions posed by Schroeder in 'entering someone else's garden'.
2. How does this metaphor resonate with you?
3. Write your personal response to each question and discuss with others how it might inform your approach to an immersion experience.
4. What opportunities does it offer for you?
5. What challenges does it present for you?

CHAPTER 4
Immersion phase

For many people, initial experiences of the reality of life in the host community can be extremely disturbing. While the disparity in socio-economic and living conditions between Australia and Majority World countries may be evident on an intellectual level, the reality of the first-hand experience can be devastating.

Culture shock

Expectations of the immersion experience prior to the trip, even if barely formed, often clash with the reality of the actual experience, thus opening up the potential for culture shock. The impact of culture shock, along with the physical and emotional reactions people experience when placed in another culture, can be unpredictable and disorienting. Observing aspects of life in another culture such as poverty, minimal educational facilities, lack of basic health care and infrastructure, and the coexistence of the extremes of wealth and poverty, can often make participants feel anxious or disturbed.

The impact of initial exposure will be different for different group members, and may surface at different times. Culture shock can be debilitating and needs to be managed carefully and skilfully by group leaders. Setting aside time for individual and group discussion and reflection can be of assistance in supporting participants through this unsettling time.

Transformative elements of immersion

Immersions, by their very nature, are complex, multi-faceted experiences which have the potential to alter the lives of participants in profound and ongoing ways. The encounter with 'otherness' is unique to each individual, and assumptions cannot be made with respect to personal responses. What may be an intense and highly significant encounter for one person, may go completely unnoticed by another.

Catalysts for such experiences are diverse and often occur as a result of incidental personal interactions between participants and the people in the host community. For many individuals, there is a defining moment that can be identified as being a 'turning point' that may trigger changes in outlook or perspectives; a point at which previously held beliefs and views of the world are challenged. For some, the shift is immediate and epochal and they can never again view the world in quite the same way. For others, the change is incremental, where one experience builds upon another, resulting in a gradual revelation of 'new dawnings'.

Immersions, by their very nature, are complex, multi-faceted experiences which have the potential to alter the lives of participants in profound and ongoing ways...

While each encounter is intensely personal, there are several elements of immersion, which if taken into account in the planning phase, are more likely to foster transformative outcomes for participants. These elements are:

- an authentic encounter with the host community
- situating the immersion within a meaningful context
- providing opportunities for reflection and debriefing
- a supportive like-minded group
- safety and wellbeing

Authentic encounter

An authentic encounter involves direct personal engagement with, and insight into, the lives of people in the host community. This encompasses participation in day-to-day activities and routines, cultural events, religious ceremonies and sharing personal stories with an orientation of mutual respect.

Factors known to contribute to transformative outcomes are:

- a destination that takes participants as far from their known experiences as possible
- experiential learning opportunities focused on encountering 'otherness'
- intimate intercultural experiences

Even for participants who have been well briefed and prepared for their immersion trip, the jolt of the reality of life in a cross-cultural community is often unexpected and unsettling. While the disorientation can be distressing for participants, it is also recognised as being an important element of the experience. Experiencing some level of discomfort and having preconceived notions challenged are necessary components of an authentic immersion, and ultimately for transformation.

> An immersion does take you out of your comfort zone and it is good to be shaken up. It is good to be awoken and reminded of your place in the universe and this world of privilege.
>
> (Michelle, Philippines)

Michelle's reflection and those following, provide examples of the personal experiences of immersion participants. They are excerpts from interviews conducted some years after the immersion trip, and the depth and intensity of their experiences are clearly evident. All names are pseudonyms.

Physical reactions to the sensory overload of the sights, the sounds, the smells and the weather, can take participants into a setting beyond their experience, and in many cases beyond their understanding. Many struggle with the reality of inequity, and inner tensions often develop between personal beliefs in human dignity and social justice, and the jarring observations of the stark disparity between wealth and poverty. Feelings of privilege and guilt can also be difficult to accept, and there may even be tensions between personal beliefs and the structure and desired outcomes of the daily program.

Importantly, disturbances and disequilibrium are a provocation for reflection and rethinking. While possessing an awareness of poverty and living conditions in many of the host communities, engagement with first-hand experiences of the realities of life for the local people can be both challenging and enlightening. A visit to a squatter settlement provided

an opportunity for Jessie to witness the rawness of daily life for the urban poor in the Philippines.

> We went down to help with the feeding program, and most of the children lined up with only a Styrofoam cup that was falling apart. They could only get a small amount of food because that is all their broken Styrofoam cup could hold. It was heartbreaking. But you need to see it. It is those harsh realities. That is what always stands out in my mind. It was not the lack of shoes, or the lack of clothes. For me, it was the fact of not even having something to put your food in, not even having a bowl to take your bread roll home in. I just think, "Oh".
>
> (Jessie, Philippines)

Multi-faceted and multi-layered historical, political, cultural and socioeconomic factors underpin the complex issues that shape the lives of the people in the host communities. To others, these can be as bewildering as they are confronting. Deep learning resides in an intensely emotional moment which stems from various unanticipated forms of disorientation, and embracing an attentiveness to discomfort. The authentic encounter experienced by participants on short-term cross-cultural immersions is a catalyst for a profound personal narrative through which they engage with the ongoing process of transformation both on immersion and in the post-immersion phase.

It is important to note here that authentic encounters are significant, regardless of where the host community is located, when the immersion takes

Think about, talk about...

1. The story recounted by Jessie typifies the experiences of immersion participants.
2. Have you had a similar personal experience?
3. How does the experience of an authentic encounter shift your view of the world?

place, or the age, gender or sending school of participants. It would seem that the depth of the engagement with the people in the host community is the important factor. Respect for the personal journeys of participants, and engaging them in encounters that promote individual and communal growth through deep learning, are at the heart of authentic immersion experience.

A meaningful context

Setting the context for an immersion experience during the preparation session is critical in increasing the likelihood of long-term change. Educating participants about the political, historical and cultural factors that contribute to the extreme poverty experienced by those living in the host community, supports this process. The inclusion of contextual factors that enable participants to draw upon personal experiences, provides points of connection and familiarity during the confrontation and disorientation of the authentic encounter.

Catholic context

Situating an immersion experience within a Catholic context provides meaningful opportunities for participants to engage with the tradition in a different cultural setting. While the expression of Catholicism in the host community may be different, it is nonetheless the same tradition, and provides participants with the opportunity to reflect on its place in their own lives.

There are many in Catholic school settings who are not affiliated with a worshipping community, and a number are not of the Catholic faith. A Catholic immersion experience can therefore have a role to play, at the very least, in assisting Catholic school community members to consider the impact of the Catholic tradition in their lives. It may also assist those who are not Catholic to understand more deeply the universality of the Christian tradition.

Prayer and liturgy

Participating in Catholic prayer and liturgy in a different cultural setting and witnessing the faith of the local people and its importance in their lives in the midst of adversity, can be a powerful experience. The celebration of family and community evident during religious ceremonies, and intergenerational involvement in all aspects of liturgy, is outside the experience of most immersion participants. Many individuals are profoundly affected by attending Mass in a different culture and consider the experience to be a high point of their trip.

> When we went to Mass up in the village in the mountains ... I do not know why, but that just totally ... I was in tears. Just the whole thing; that moved me more than anything ... and there was some sort of realisation of the reason I was supposed to have been there.
>
> (Sarah, Philippines)

Think about, talk about...

1. What are some different expressions of the Catholic tradition you have observed in a cross-cultural setting?
2. How are they similar to or different from the expression of Catholic religious practice in Australia?
3. Have you recognised a spiritual dimension in your experience of immersion?

Recognising artwork, and religious symbols, quotes and prayers, and observing the expression of Catholicism in a different cultural setting deepens an understanding of the tradition. It also provides points of connection within the group and to the host community; it offers a bridge between participants' own past experiences and how they might integrate new understandings into their personal, professional and spiritual lives.

Personal spirituality

As well as evoking a physical and emotional response, and engaging participants in personal and professional learning, immersion experiences have the capacity to profoundly touch the spirit. Opportunities arise for people to involve themselves in personal and shared religious experiences, and to reflect upon their own spirituality in a different cultural context.

As spirituality is a uniquely individual journey, different trigger points emerge for connecting to personal beliefs and ideologies. Many find immersions to be a powerful expression of Catholicism, while those who are not Catholic often discover the experience to be spiritual in a different sense. Some have a profound response to witnessing the faith and devotional practices of the local people, and feel a deep spiritual connection to the communities they visit. Others find themselves unexpectedly stirred by inspiration and hope, while for some participants, there is no discernible spiritual aspect to the experience at all.

> At one point, Sister Grazia then led the Rosary. It was one of the top three moments of my spiritual life, I would have to say. It was one of the most moving things I have ever experienced, and it just took me to another level.
>
> (Nina, Philippines)

> I had a strong sense of [the] presence of God on the trip, but a lot of questions about the presence of the Church. And coming back it has deepened my sense of the spiritual that is in people of all places and cultures.
>
> (Olivia, Kiribati)

> The Mass at the beginning in Manila, I felt ... I mean, I have gone to church my whole

While the hymns and prayers are usually in the language of the host community, the ritual provides a sense of familiarity and certainty. Immersion participants are often moved by the congregation's enthusiasm and fervour and by watching rituals such as children presenting agricultural produce from family gardens during the Offertory Procession at Mass; and later seeing that same produce prepared by the women for the visitors' morning tea. Witnessing family and community participation in religious ceremonies in another culture somehow seems to reinforce the significance of what has been lost at home.

life, but I do not go anywhere near Mass on a Sunday now, but that was beautiful.
(Imogen, Philippines)

Many immersion participants are profoundly moved by their spiritual experiences and continue to explore dimensions of personal spirituality after returning home. Others are touched by a sense of inspiration and hope in the lives of the local people, and a recognition of missionary discipleship through those who have come to live and work in the host communities.

Not that spiritual so much, for me, just ... I suppose more an inspiration, and maybe to reflect on, "Okay so in my life what am I going to respond to? What am I going to do?" (Sam, Philippines)

Setting the immersion within the meaningful context of the Catholic tradition promotes opportunities for engagement with deeper levels of spiritual awareness and theological understanding while on immersion. Although many participants are moved by participation in religious ritual and prayer during an immersion, it is unclear whether this translates to increased involvement in a worshipping community after returning home.

Reflection and debriefing

Reflection and debriefing are recognised as being integral to transformation. The reflection component of immersion allows individuals to deepen the process of formation by making meaning of the experience in their lives.

You are grounded consistently with that daily reflection and debrief, absolutely wonderful and a necessity.
(Mike, Philippines)

Along with guided and shared reflection, is the need of some participants for quiet, personal space in order to make meaning of their experiences.

I wanted quiet time after some of those experiences. I just needed that space; some people need that.
(Rosanna, Philippines)

It is important to offer a range of opportunities for debriefing and reflection. Some people appreciate group discussions and benefit from hearing the reflections of others, as it helps to validate their own thoughts and feelings. Others do not feel comfortable contributing to discussions and prefer quiet reflection and journaling. Still others choose a creative path through which to make meaning of their experience. This may take various forms such as sketching, photography, poetry or music.

Different prayer styles such as *Lectio Divina* and *Visio Divina* have also been found to be a powerful way to assist in the reflective process. As individuals experience immersion differently, and are at various stages of the 'journey' at different times, it is important that opportunities for a range of different styles of reflection and debriefing are offered and modelled

Think about, talk about…

1. What style of debriefing are you most drawn to?
2. What other types of debriefing methods have you used with immersion participants?
3. How might these methods support participants as they search for meaning from their experiences of immersion?

at regular intervals. It is also important that there is a clear alignment between the methods and processes of reflective practice, and the context and rationale of the immersion.

A supportive group

An immersion, particularly in the early stages, or after a disturbing encounter, can be a source of intense disorientation which can leave people feeling helpless, vulnerable and emotional. Being able to debrief with a supportive like-minded group which shares a common understanding of immersion, and which might provide ongoing support throughout the time away, is of great importance.

Providing opportunities to engage in formal and informal discussions with others in the group allows participants to explore this 'misfit' in a safe and supportive space. It is through this process that experiences are reflected upon, assumptions and beliefs are challenged and meaning can be understood. As such, it is essential to establish routines and structures that are conducive to open, safe and supportive dialogue in the initial stages of an immersion.

Safety and wellbeing

For many participants to be able to fully engage in the immersion experience, personal safety and security are of high importance. The presence of organisational features and attention to detail in the planning phase help to avoid the barriers to transformation that occur when programs are less structured.

Clarity of purpose, briefing and debriefing sessions, feeling safe, having confidence in the coordinators' ability to lead the trip, and a balanced itinerary which includes a range of cultural activities, are essential components. For most participants, an immersion trip

Think about, talk about…

1. How might you go about building a sense of community within your immersion group to best enable a climate of freedom and support?
2. How might you begin this process in the pre-immersion phase and during the immersion itself?

is their first encounter with a Majority World culture, and feeling secure and confident in an unfamiliar setting alleviates some level of anxiety and allows them to freely engage in the experience.

> We stayed in a place where we felt safe and comfortable, so that we actually had energy to be able to pour into absorbing this experience. I think that was really important ... I thought that made it possible to actually process things a bit better.
> (Angie, Philippines)

While some level of discomfort is an inevitable, and indeed necessary, aspect of an immersion trip, an experience that is too overwhelming may trigger an emotive need for personal security. The significance attached to feeling physically and emotionally safe in a confronting and unfamiliar cross-cultural environment has important implications for organising entities in terms of assessment and management of risk factors relating to immersion trips.

The safety and wellbeing of people in the host community is also an important consideration. Along with the potential for overburdening fragile communities, knowledge of risk factors concerning appropriate relationships, safeguarding and the responsible use of social media need to be high on the agenda, particularly when managing student groups on immersion.

Organisational features are central to all elements of immersion in fostering transformative outcomes. Situating an immersion within a meaningful context, providing opportunities for an authentic encounter, the regular provision of a range of opportunities for reflection and debriefing, building a community

Think about, talk about…

1. What measures might you put into place to safeguard the wellbeing of participants on your immersion trip?
2. The safety and wellbeing of the host community also needs to be considered in your planning. What strategies could you put in place to support this?

culture of support within the group, and managing the safety and well-being of participants and the host community, are all features of immersion trips which are the responsibility of organisers.

If organising entities seek to foster transformative outcomes in participants through immersion, then it is incumbent upon them to ensure the provision of such opportunities in the design and facilitation of the trip.

Organisational features are central to all elements of immersion in fostering transformative outcomes...

CHAPTER 5
Post-immersion phase

The immersion experience does not end after arriving back home. In the post-immersion phase, schools and organising entities have further responsibilities. These include assisting participants to navigate the re-entry phase, the provision of opportunities for ongoing reflection and debriefing, and guiding participants towards appropriate initiatives for action. Responsibilities also include debriefing with the host community and looking at ways to further develop and strengthen the partnership.

Reverse culture shock, also known as 're-entry shock' or 'own culture shock' is also a significant factor. This is particularly relevant in the case of short-term immersions, where participants have barely come to terms with the encounter of life in another culture with all its complexities, and they have to return to the stark reality of their own. This period of adjustment can be a very unsettling experience as the symptoms of disorientation and feelings of helplessness are similar to those of culture shock itself.

Generally speaking, there is a high correlation between age and experience, and re-entry shock. An important consideration for those organising immersion experiences for students is that reverse culture shock tends to be much more prevalent in younger people. Also of interest is that those who adjust to the host culture with relative ease, tend to find it more difficult to readjust to their own culture after returning home and may experience a greater degree of re-entry shock.

Predictably, the longer the period of time away, the greater the level of re-entry shock, and those having higher levels of communication and engagement with people in the host community will more likely experience a greater degree of re-entry shock. Also of significance for organisers, is that individuals who have had previous cross-cultural experience have less re-entry shock than those who have not been on an immersion before.

In most cases, there is a significant shift within a very short period of time, and there is an evident self-awareness around the need to process individual responses to the immersion. Collectively, participants generally feel a strong need to respond to their experience through some form of action, particularly action that influences others.

In the short term

In the short term, (generally within three months of returning from an immersion trip), participants primarily engage in navigating the re-entry period, re-evaluating their lifestyle and reporting back to their schools.

Re-entry is a critical time for participants in making sense of their experience post-immersion. The dissonance between the recent experience of immersion and the reality of life at home can be a particularly unsettling time for many individuals. A range of feelings such as exhilaration, exhaustion, disturbance and frustration are commonly experienced, combined with the feeling that people at home do not really understand what has happened for them. Many people also express an overwhelming desire to return to the host community.

Re-entry is a critical time for participants in making sense of their experience post-immersion...

Think about, talk about…

1. Have you had a personal experience of culture shock or re-entry shock?

2. What did it feel like? How did you overcome it?

3. An awareness of culture shock and re-entry shock is critical for immersion organisers. It will be experienced by some members of your group and may manifest itself in a variety of ways.

4. What strategies could you put into place to manage this unsettling reaction?

> I think when you first come back you are pretty fired up; you have been to the mountaintop!
>
> (Olivia, Kiribati)

> I came back in a state of lethargy. So physically it was really tiring to get up. I think it must be what depression feels like. So, the inertia of doing daily life, it felt that I was trudging through things, that I was carrying a huge weight physically, like I just felt that I had put on 25 kilos and that I was carrying a 25-kilo backpack. I did not understand what it was at the time.
>
> (Michelle, Philippines)

Critical reflection through ongoing debriefing sessions, dialogue with those who have shared the experience, and reporting back to schools, are important steps in assisting participants to make meaning of their experience.

Reassessment of lifestyle

After having been exposed to an environment which is geographically, historically, politically, culturally and economically different from their own, many immersion participants engage in critical reflection in the immediate post-immersion phase. A re-evaluation of lifestyle and priorities is a common reaction.

> I had this strange urge to de-clutter my life. I just felt like I needed to take a step back and work out what is really important in life.
>
> (Annabelle, Philippines)

> The immersion gave me the impetus to change my life. And from that personal perspective of just clearing things up, saying "You have been with people who have nothing, you are doing things that do not make you happy, go back and clean your life up". And that is pretty much what I did. And I think it took me out of being too self-aware, too selfish maybe.
>
> (Nikki, Philippines)

The reactions of Annabelle and Nikki point to a profound personal realisation triggered by their immersion. For many, the immersion experience is their first encounter with a Majority World community, and the first shocking realisation of the immense wealth and privilege of a Western lifestyle.

Think about, talk about…

1. Have you had an experience similar to those of Annabelle and Nikki after returning from an immersion trip?

2. In what other ways might a reassessment of lifestyle manifest itself in the actions of participants returning from an immersion trip?

3. What strategies might schools and organising entities put in place to support participants through the re-entry phase?

Feedback to schools

The authentic encounter of immersion can leave participants feeling powerless and ineffectual. Formal and informal opportunities for talking about their experiences to schools and community groups can provide important avenues for them to be able to engage in action and advocacy, and to make meaning of their experiences.

Formal reporting back to schools involves facilitating presentations to leadership teams, staff meetings, student year groups and house groups, and even to whole school assemblies and parent groups. There is great value in reporting back in terms of awareness raising and strengthening links between schools and host communities. The critical reflection required in the preparation of presentations to school communities also supports participants in the transformative process.

Informal conversations with supportive staff members, students, family and friends also offer important ways for participants to debrief. Continuing to talk with others who have a shared experience of immersion is critical in the initial weeks after returning home. Another motivation for reporting back to schools is a sense of responsibility to tell the stories of the people in the host communities.

> If you are going to go and walk in host communities like that, you have a moral imperative to make a difference somehow when you come back.
>
> (Mike, Philippines)

In the busyness of school life and crowded agendas for staff meetings and assemblies, the opportunity to report back is sometimes lost, leaving participants feeling disappointed and somewhat inadequate. All styles of debriefing offering critical reflection on the immersion experience appear to be useful in the transformative process. However, schools need to be clear about who is responsible for organising the presentation of a report on the experience. Reporting back directly at system level or to school boards may be other possible avenues for consideration.

In summary, re-entry is an extremely significant time for participants. Reflecting critically on the immersion through ongoing debriefing sessions, and initiating conversations with those who have shared the experience, are important steps in assisting them to make meaning of the experience. Organising entities and school and system leadership teams have a substantive role to play in supporting participants through the process of critical reflection post-immersion. This role involves facilitating a range of opportunities for debriefing and feedback. Clarity around role responsibilities in this regard is of high importance.

In the medium term

The medium term can be said to encompass the timeframe of between three and 18 months after returning from an immersion trip. After additional time for reflection, there is an increased awareness in most participants that the impact of their immersion does not dissipate, and there is a heightened appreciation of the possibility of being an advocate for meaningful change.

> You feel pretty passionate, like you want to change the world when you come back from a trip like that.
>
> (Imogen, Philippines)

Whether initially feeling euphoric, disillusioned, anxious or overwhelmed, a need to engage in some form of action begins to surface and take shape in

Think about, talk about…

1. What strategies might your school develop to ensure opportunities for formal and informal debriefing and feedback are provided for participants in the post-immersion phase?

2. What structures already present in your school support this process?

3. Can you identify structures that may need to be further developed in order to support this process?

the medium term. What the particular course of action might involve is not always immediately apparent, however, although the evolving plan is generally aimed at influencing others in some way.

Volunteering

The immersion experience stimulates a desire in participants to do something more with their lives and to respond to their experience in some practical way. It may even be seen as providing a missing piece in a person's life.

> The Philippines experience really inspired me and gave me the internal drive to want to have more of that experience. So, I went to Timor for a week later that year and in the following year for three months, and since then I have actively sought out other agencies and ways I could do work like that. So, I did a trip to Vietnam and Cambodia with a group of students for a month. I have also been involved for the last four years with the Australian Catholic University helping run a community sports program in Baucau, East Timor.
>
> (Leah, Philippines)

While volunteering overseas is a profoundly life-changing experience, many participants make small, quiet adjustments in areas such as thinking more carefully about integrating changes to their patterns of donating to charities.

> And so, very quietly now, I am very conscious of, if I am giving particularly financial support, that it goes somewhere that is really going to make a difference.
>
> (Mark, Philippines)

Volunteering abroad and changed altruistic behaviour are significant outcomes attributed directly to immersion experiences. It may be that individuals who put themselves forward for immersion trips are more attracted to this type of activity and possess a certain predisposition for the experience in the first place. While such actions may have previously appealed to participants, it is likely that the catalyst for change was missing. In many cases, people have been searching for something more in their lives, and the immersion experience provides an avenue for them to further explore that desire in a very practical way. These types of significant actions are indeed 'life-changing' and indicate a deep and profound level of ongoing transformation.

The pivotal nature of the medium-term timeframe

The medium term is a pivotal timeframe. It is during this period that most participants engage in some form of action that involves influencing others in their school community. They have negotiated the re-entry phase and have returned to life, work and school commitments, yet would seem to remain highly motivated by their immersion experience to become architects of change.

After returning home, most people express the desire to 'give back' in some way and this aspiration is realised by various means. Individual capacity for action would seem to be dictated by personal life and work circumstances and usually takes place within an individual's sphere of influence within their school community.

Plans for strengthening partnerships with the host community evolve into awareness raising and fund raising, and personal transformation becomes a catalyst for influencing the lives of others, particularly in the professional sphere. As the re-entry phase is often a period of further disorientation and readjustment for participants, the increased clarity gained from further reflection and dialogue in the short term makes the medium-term timeframe more conducive to sustained and significant plans for action.

The possibility for long-term change increases if immersion participants are involved in action and advocacy after returning home. Importantly for schools and organisers, they require explicit guidance at this time on how to enact new understandings and aspirations.

Through the experience of immersion, participants often come to the realisation that their personal values are in fact very closely aligned with the ethos of their school community, and that the internalisation of this realisation comes to fruition in the medium term. It is incumbent upon schools and organising entities to ensure support for participants during this period, and to channel the individual's energy and enthusiasm into actions which are:

1. developed in dialogue with the host community
2. aimed at strengthening partnerships between the school community and the host community
3. undertaken collectively rather than individually
4. focused on enhancing missionary discipleship

Advice and direction for participants in relation to these factors is crucial. Consideration of the potential for damage to fragile host communities through uninformed, albeit well-intentioned activists, is imperative. As impulsive, emotive reactions are more likely in the exuberance of the short-term timeframe, channelling (or even curbing) energy and enthusiasm derived from an immersion participant's 'new dawnings' may well be the key to supporting and promoting the Catholic Social Teaching dimension of subsidiarity, and developing in participants the desirable long-term attributes of:

1. attitudes that stem from informed rather than privileged perspectives

2. dispositions that preference dialogue over assumptions

3. partnerships with host-communities that are equal and mutually beneficial, rather than those which are unilateral and encourage an unhealthy dependency

The medium term is the timeframe during which participants are most likely to engage in action. It is a time of high energy and high enthusiasm. In the school setting, a supportive environment that nurtures an individual's plan for action encourages transformative process.

In the long term

The impact of an immersion experience remains strong in the lives of participants many years after the event, and is often described as being a lifelong change in the way they view the world. While engagement in action triggered by the immersion would seem to be more measured with the passing of time, so too do the outcomes of the experience become deeply embedded and different realisations emerge.

> It is life-altering in a sense that at the most opportune and inopportune moments in the rest of your life, something will come back of that experience that then will help you to discern what is happening for you in the present. I imagine that that is going to be there for the rest of my life.
>
> (Gina, Philippines)

In the longer term, participants have had more time to engage in critical reflection and to consider an appropriate timeframe in which to act upon their

post-immersion aspirations. Rather than acting on impulse or in a tokenistic way, they take a more considered approach and often come to realise they would be able to make a more substantial contribution to a path such as volunteer work at a different stage in their life.

When aspiration is present it points to the search for something more in life, which mirrors the initial trigger for many to go on an immersion in the first place. Some people find they are somewhat constrained by life circumstances and not able to fulfil their aspirations until many years later when more appropriate life circumstances can be facilitated.

> It has taken me a very long time, and a lot of that is practical, raising kids and looking after parents, and all of that. So maybe, now there is a bit more space in my life, this is really starting to bubble up a lot more now. So, it is an aspiration, and a yearning that whatever the next chapter of my life will be, it will in some way involve some advocacy or activism.
>
> (Gina, Philippines)

The transformative process after an immersion experience is profound, deep and ongoing. After negotiating the re-entry phase in the short term and the high-energy, high-activity period of the medium term, the long-term timeframe is a more reflective phase during which a clearer perspective about the meaning of the immersion is gained. The experience never leaves participants and it often becomes a reference point for important decisions later in life.

Think about, talk about...

The actual needs of the host community do not always align with the needs perceived by immersion participants.

What aspects might you need to consider in relation to best supporting both the enthusiasm of immersion participants and the actual needs of the host community?

The impact of an immersion experience remains strong in the lives of participants many years after the event...

CHAPTER 6
Immersion and formation

Essentially, the Catholic school is called to be a living witness of the love of God among us. It can, moreover, become a means through which it is possible to discern, in the light of the Gospel, what is positive in the world, what needs to be transformed and what injustices must be overcome.[6]

Formation is therefore central to the ongoing life and mission of Catholic schools. So that all school community members may deepen their knowledge and understanding of God's mission, provision of appropriate opportunities for formation is a priority for Catholic educational authorities.

The word formation refers to "a set of experiences designed to prepare a person or group for a particular purpose".[7] Essentially, the purpose of formation is "to invite all those involved in educational ministry to be anchored in a Catholic vision that is personal and public, reflective and active, nurturing and transformative".[8]

A contemporary understanding of formation is that it is an invitation to participate in God's mission in the world today. Formation for mission is therefore 'Christ-centred'. It is an intentional, ongoing and reflective process that focuses on the growth of individuals and communities from their lived experiences, in spiritual awareness, theological understanding, vocational motivation and capabilities for mission and service in the Church and the world.[4]

This view of formation recognises the diversity of populations within and across Catholic schools, and underscores the need for re-imagining possibilities for flexible delivery of formation programs as exemplified by short-term cross-cultural immersions.

Deepening a shared understanding of values, ethos and mission through an invitational approach is at the heart of formation for Catholic schools. Short-term cross-cultural immersion makes a substantial contribution to this process. Experiences have a profound and ongoing impact on the lives of participants, causing them to re-perceive and re-place themselves in the world. The experiential nature of the trips engages participants personally in the stories of their tradition, their school and the host communities, thereby enhancing the possibility for transformation.

Potential for teachers

Immersions have the potential to change teachers' perspectives about themselves and about the vocation of teaching. Having the opportunity to observe and participate in teaching and learning in a different cultural setting provides unforeseen insight into their profession. The benefits of immersion trips extend well beyond cross-cultural and global competencies. In fact they extend to influencing the very heart of teachers' beliefs about education and about themselves as teachers.

> I think it changed forever in me, things about my view of the value of education. It profoundly struck me that education is the only way that society can change.
>
> (Sam, Philippines)

Along with lifestyle changes, teachers who go on immersions feel compelled to make meaningful changes in their workplace. Common reactions include a deeper understanding of and connection to their school community, as well as to mission and justice initiatives.

> It gave me the confidence to then want to further my career in that school, and stay in that school, and value my job, and want to be part of that community.
>
> (Nikki, Philippines)

> The immersion definitely also catapulted me into being more involved in the formation and mission side of the school. I just felt more natural in that space.
>
> (Nina, Philippines)

> Before the trip, the work of mission in the school had no connection to me, it was just in one ear and out the other. Social Justice Day and social justice activities and Reflection Days were quite painful for me before. They were annoyances because they kept me from what I perceived to be my job, as being a deliverer of content and skills in Science.
>
> Whereas, when it came around this year, I thought, "I am a part of Social Justice Day". I am not the teacher complaining, "I am missing a Science lesson with my Year 12s." Now I have realised that curriculum sits side by side with my job of delivering a social justice message. It also gave me a new appreciation of teachers of Religion and the work of the Social Justice team. Yes, so I am a convert!
>
> (Chris, Timor-Leste)

The shift in attitude described by Nikki, Nina and Chris underscores the powerful potential of immersion in the formation of staff. This shift is echoed by many others who look for ways to involve themselves in the mission life of their school in the post-immersion phase. Increased involvement in student retreats and reflection days is also a common outcome said to have been triggered by an immersion experience.

Teachers who have been on immersion often gain greater knowledge and understanding of their school's founding story, values and ethos. This in turn gives them increased confidence and involvement in the mission life of the school. It may also be that the search for the 'missing piece' in their lives leads participants to actions relating to mission and service. Increased commitment to the school community and to social justice initiatives are also key indicators of "growth in individuals from their lived experiences", and indeed, highly desirable outcomes of formation programs.

Associated with staff becoming more aligned to their school communities after immersion, and making substantial contributions in areas of school life they

Think about, talk about…

1. How has the experience of immersion influenced your professional life?
2. Has your view of teaching as a profession and as a vocation changed in some way after an experience of immersion?

had not previously been involved in, is the role of the school community itself in nurturing and supporting these contributions.

Potential for school communities

One cannot over-estimate the value of immersion participants returning to a supportive work or school community which provides regular opportunities for them to reconnect, and reignite their experience in different ways. The significance of a supportive school community after returning home aligns seamlessly with being part of a supportive group while on the immersion itself. Connection and commitment of individuals to the school and to God's mission are strengthened as a result of this approach.

The experience of immersion builds confidence and aspirations in participants. It engenders in them a desire to personally engage in the process again, and a desire to influence others to do the same. Many participants desire to return to the same host community and establish personal relationships with members of that community. Others plan to facilitate a similar experience for family, friends, other staff members or students.

Immersion trips also have the potential to shift a school's culture. When greater numbers of school community members have been involved in immersion trips there are higher levels of 'buy-in' and, subsequently, less resistance to the implementation of mission initiatives across the school community. The effect of immersion continues well beyond the individual and leads to growth of the school community.

Formation of staff and students in the values, traditions and ethos of a school works towards building a supportive school culture. The desire of participants to engage in some form of action that influences others after their experience, has a synergistic effect that encourages involvement of the wider school community in mission and justice initiatives.

> It is that idea of developing not just a civil society, but a civil and a just society, and I do think it makes an enormous difference to a school community. And if you have got a critical mass it is a lot easier.
> (Heath, Western Australia)

As participants are transformed by their personal encounter they feel compelled to engage in action that influences others. When a number of members of staff and students from the same school have been involved in immersion trips, the collective capacity for shifting the culture of the school community increases, particularly in relation to mission. Enhanced understanding of, and commitment to, the values and ethos of the school and increased levels of engagement in activities relating to the mission life of the school, are outcomes of immersion which have a significant impact on the wider school community, and go to the very heart of Catholic education.

The effect of immersion continues well beyond the individual and leads to growth of the school community...

Think about, talk about...

1. In what ways has your school been influenced by the actions of immersion participants?
2. How has the mission life of the school been changed or enhanced by these actions?

CHAPTER 7
Immersion and transformation

Transformation has been described as one of the most powerful words in the English language. The basis of transformative learning is a "dramatic, fundamental change in the way we see ourselves and the world in which we live". The deep learning gained from involvement in short-term cross-cultural immersion operates as a catalyst for internal shifts, and changed perspectives and behaviours.

For deep and ongoing personal transformation to occur, sociologist John Mezirow[9] maintains individuals need to move through four distinct phases:

1. the experience of a disorienting dilemma
2. critical reflection on that experience
3. rational discourse with others who have shared the experience
4. engagement in some form of action as a response to the experience

All of these aspects of personal transformation are present in authentic, well-planned immersion experiences. These transformational changes may be epochal or incremental. An epochal transformation as is often experienced in an immersion context, is a sudden dramatic reorienting insight that challenges a person's core identity.

> It somehow leaves you with a bit of an impression that you cannot ever see the world in quite the same way that you saw it before. For most people, there is a moment where something happens. It might not have actually been noticed by anybody else, but for that person this is that moment where there is some shift, and I think the long-term impact of that is probably incalculable. I think if you have actually had that moment, if you are open to that moment, then that changes everything, because you cannot ever quite go back to what you were before.
>
> (Gerry, Philippines)

As the purpose of formation is transformation of individuals and communities, it is important to consider the elements of immersion that have been found to foster or promote transformative outcomes.

Immersion experiences provide opportunities for transformative learning as people are placed outside of daily routines and into an orientation of 'otherness', both geographically and culturally. Travel researcher Susan Ross[10] maintains the elements of immersion which increase opportunities for transformation are:

1. a destination that pulls the individual as far as possible from known experiences
2. intimate intercultural experiences involving in-depth discussions

Think about, talk about...

1. Have you ever had an experience of an epochal transformational change on an immersion trip?
2. How were you changed by the experience?

3. activities that stimulate contemplation resulting in meaning-making of the experiences
4. post-travel activities that help participants to continue to reflect upon and extract meaning from the experience

These insights are very helpful in planning immersion experiences. The more different geographically and culturally the host community is, the more likely it is that transformation will take place. The stronger the sense of being an outsider, the more likely the occurrence of disorientation will be. Transformation is also more likely to occur if one has the opportunity to reflect on their experience either individually or collectively. Immersion experiences should therefore be intentionally designed to be transformative, and to allow time and space for critical reflection.

The provision of opportunities for reflection and debriefing during and after an immersion is pivotal to the experience, and provides critical pathways to transformation. It has been noted that people need to be led through their experiences to consciously understand the meaning and impact on their lives.

Think about, talk about…

1. Which of the transformative elements of immersion listed above are currently present in the experiences you plan and provide?
2. Which do you consider to be the most important?
3. How might knowledge of these transformative elements inform your future planning?

CHAPTER 8
Theological reflection for mission

The events encountered on an immersion trip are, in many ways, beyond the experience and understanding of most participants. The multi-faceted and multi-layered historical, political, cultural and socioeconomic factors that underpin the complex issues that shape the lives of the people in the host community can be as bewildering as they are confronting. It is critical then that participants are offered direction in making meaning of what they have seen, heard and felt while on immersion. Guiding people through a process which involves the convergence of life experience and the spiritual journey demands recognition of its innate individuality, complexity and diversity. The art of theological reflection is a straightforward yet powerful reflective process, which goes to the heart of 'being' and of 'doing' mission.

The significant number of models of theological reflection that have been developed over time have several features in common. Essentially, participants are led through a process in which human experience is interpreted in light of the faith tradition, leading to transformation and action.

The type of event or life experience being considered informs the selection of the most appropriate model of theological reflection. Flexibility and creativity are central to the effective application of any model, as the 'one size fits all' approach is neither helpful nor useful.

The method suggested for use in relation to immersion experiences is an adaptation of John Trokan's *Models of Theological Reflection: Theory and Praxis*.[11] Trokan's work draws primarily on the work of Whitehead and Whitehead.[12]

Trokan sees theological reflection as a powerful and growth-filled tool in several ways as it:

- stands in the personal experience of each individual and reverences that experience as spiritual

- examines the Christian Scriptures to uncover its truth for contemporary experience

- befriends the Christian tradition to filter out its history and wisdom for contemporary culture

- critically examines the personal, family, and cultural contexts which have been formational in a person's values, beliefs, and theology

- develops the discipline of an action-reflection process of theologising and discernment

- enables the individual to experience the process of theology as a communal enterprise, which models various faith responses to significant events.

Recalling significant events, such as those experienced on an immersion trip, and interpreting their meaning, assists participants in identifying the wisdom of their cultural and faith traditions. Theological reflection also enables people to recognise and explicitly name the beliefs and values which shape their worldview. This self-awareness is a catalyst for ongoing integration of learning in heads, hearts and hands; and ultimately for transformation for mission.

Trokan's model of theological reflection involves five phases – retrieving, retelling, reframing, reconnecting and re-visioning.

In adapting Trokan's model to the context of an immersion trip, the first phase consists of retrieving a significant event experienced during an immersion. The second phase involves retelling the event in story form to a small group. In phase three the experience is reframed in the large group, and phase four

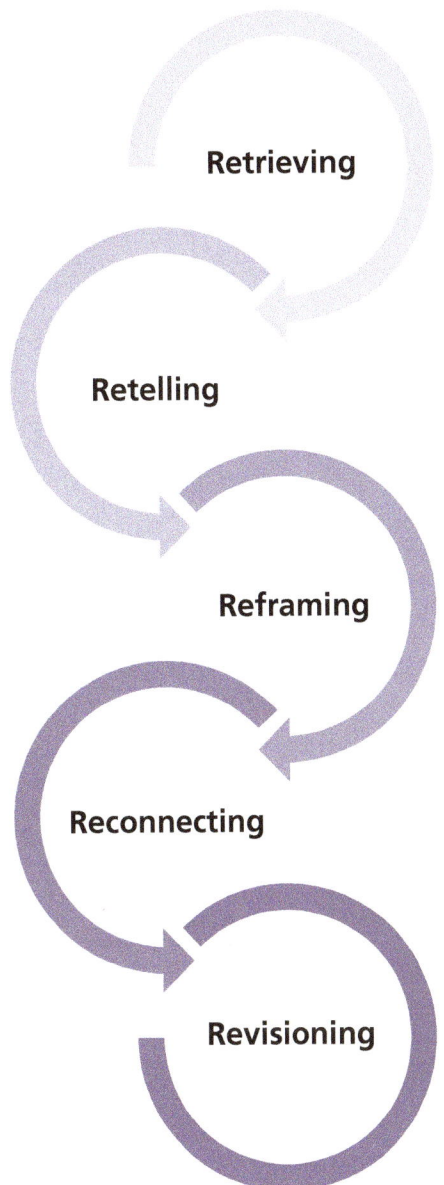

Figure 7: Trokan's Praxis of Theological Reflection

reconnects the experience to the Christian story. The final phase involves re-visioning the experience through the new perspective, and focusing on an appropriate decision, response or action.

The phases of the model are outlined below and examples of personal experiences are included.

1. Retrieving

At the outset, the model seeks to encourage participants to remember an experience they encountered whilst on an immersion trip. Initially, this is prompted by guiding questions to lead them back to the experience.

Consider the following questions:

- Recall a significant event that occurred on an immersion trip:
    - That was a 'light-bulb' moment for you?
    - Where you felt changed or transformed?
    - Where you felt the presence of God?

- Recall the setting of the event:
    - What was the day like?
    - The time?
    - The weather?
    - The sights, sounds and smells?

- Recall the context of the event:
  - When did it happen?
  - Where were you?
  - Why were you there?
  - Who were you with?
  - What were the conversations and interactions related to the event?
  - What were your feelings when it happened?
  - Why is the experience significant for you?

> We walked in through these tiny little alleyways to get to someone's house. I remember it was so stinking hot, it was dripping. When we were coming back out again, we heard a baby crying and some girls said to us, "Come in, come in, here is a new-born baby." There, on the dirt floor of this tiny little hot, hot, sauna-like hot shanty, was a lady who had just given birth. She was just lying there exhausted, with all these other women around her. So that was just, "Wow!!" Again, it was another one of those moments. It was just like, "I cannot believe this!"
>
> (Leah, Philippines)

Reliving an immersion event takes group members back to the experience 'in a heart-beat'. Including a sensory component brings it into even sharper focus, as recalling the physical reaction stimulates memories generated by the head and heart. For many participants, the jolt of the reality of life in a Majority World context is often as unexpected as it is unsettling. Factors such as population density, poverty and lack of health-care facilities can have an immediate and profoundly disturbing impact.

Group members may choose to recall their experience through their imaginations, or to relive the memory creatively through journaling, poetry, music or art. They are encouraged to reconnect with the experience without limits or judgments. Regardless of the nature of the experience, the aim here is to enable participants to re-engage freely with the experience.

2. Retelling

After recalling the experience individually, group members then move to smaller breakout groups of two or three people, to retell their stories. The act of sharing stories enables participants to "experience theology as an activity of people which is communal, conversational, and ongoing".

There are two important elements in this phase — storytelling and story listening.

- Storytelling:
  - Group members are invited in turn to retell their experiences in as much detail as they can without interruption, interpretation or judgment.
  - Participants then have the opportunity to share why the experience is significant for them and what it means for them.

- Story listening:
  - Listening attentively to another allows a person to enter into their world and to understand the world as he or she does.
  - Giving another our undivided attention assists in connecting people more deeply with the presence of God.[13]

> One thing that was very important in our group was that people felt that they could be emotional in front of each other. It would be terrible to have a group you did not feel comfortable with, and at the same time confront these feelings that you have. So, it is pretty important that the group 'gets' you.
>
> (Sam, Philippines)

Being part of a supportive group and feeling comfortable and emotionally safe within that group allows deeper layers of meaning to emerge. At the time the event occurred, a sense of the sacred may not have been apparent. Its retelling opens the possibility for graced moments and 'kingdom spaces' which enliven the Spirit within us.

3. Reframing

After retelling their stories in small groups, participants regather as a larger group. During this phase of reflection, they are led through a reconstruction of their experiences from a theological perspective. This involves providing a lens through which seemingly ordinary human experiences become clearly and profoundly spiritual.

Consider the following questions:

- In relation to your personal wisdom:
  - What does the experience mean for you?
  - What do the remembering and retelling of the event do to you internally?
  - Why is the experience significant for you?

- In relation to the wisdom of the faith tradition:
  - What values are important for you as you recall the experience?
  - What do you believe in light of the experience?
  - What is 'of God' in all this?
  - What images of God, Jesus and Church surface from this reflection?

During this phase each participant describes their own perception of the event. As the meaning and learnings are interpreted in the group context, a fundamental theological truth emerges:

> to stand in one another's experiences is to walk on holy ground. This is sacred space for the individual as well as for the community that recognises this is God's space, where God continues to walk and operate. Each of these stories is significant, for they reveal how God continues to contact us. The theological task is to tease out the underlying foundational convictions and permanent attitudes which have been implicitly learned from the experience and to make them explicit.

> My memory is that the experience was spiritual for me in a very raw sense. Which is what I think, spirituality should be. It does make you question ... when you see a child on the street in Manila sleeping, it is confronting in a spiritual sense of, how come God chose for me to be born in such a privileged world and what is my responsibility then, to my brothers and sisters on the other side of the globe?
> (Angie, Philippines)

The facilitator and other group members assist participants to make meaning of their experiences. Reframing in a group setting enables participants to see how others have interpreted their immersion experiences through a spiritual lens and integrated them into a process of personal and ongoing conversion of life.

4. Reconnecting

After sharing and reframing their story, group members are encouraged to connect to the Christian story. In the current Australian Catholic landscape, biblical illiteracy and a detraditionalised world present complex challenges and opportunities for facilitators of theological reflection. As some people may feel overwhelmed and not know where to begin, appropriate examples may need to be provided for them to select from. The aim in this phase centres on fostering and nurturing both "critical awareness of, and comfort with the diverse testimony of scripture and tradition".

When guided to reflect upon an image from the faith tradition that emerges from their reflection, an individual's ordinary experience is translated into explicit theological language and concepts so that attitudes and perceptions of their immersion are reframed.

Consider the following questions:

- Is there a story or image from the Christian tradition that comes to mind in relation to the event you have remembered?

- Is there a message or insight you can draw from this story or image in relation to your experience?

> The Sisters are just amazing. I think walking into the Community Centre, walking into the Kinder School and seeing how they live out the Parable of the Good Samaritan in really, really practical ways; it just makes the story come alive. They are the Good Samaritan and Jesus in those places. The

way that they give such dignity to these people and they do not discriminate. They give dignity and hope to anyone who is in need. I just saw Jesus in these people.

(Maddie, Philippines)

"Go and do likewise". They just do it. They see a need, they have gone and done it. And they are continually doing it. It is not static. It is such a dynamic process. There is always something new starting, whether it be visiting prisons or the shanties or things within the Kinder School. They are living out that Gospel through and through, 100%!!

(Jack, Philippines)

This phase also leads participants into broader questions for theological reflection. Experiencing the Catholic tradition in another cultural context leads to questions of what it means for us as community locally and globally, what it means for discipleship from a Christological perspective, and what God's mission is calling us to. When intertwined with the Christian story, the deeply confronting and disturbing events experienced on an immersion trip become portals to kingdom spaces, to liberation and to evangelisation.

5. Revisioning

In the final phase of revisioning, participants move towards a response, a decision or an action, which becomes a catalyst for a fundamental shift in the way they view the world. Conversion is "a re-centring of personal identity" or "a depth response to change at the core of the human person" This conversion or transformation causes many to re-evaluate lifestyle choices and to 're-perceive' and 're-place' themselves in the world. It is about recognising the presence of God in all things.

Consider the following questions:

- Is there a decision, an action or a response that you feel drawn to as a result of your reflection?
- Are there practical considerations that need to be taken into account in actioning your response?
- Are there others who might need to be considered or consulted?
- How would God's mission be enlivened by your plan?

Elements of Catholic Social Teaching help to inform a response to a theological reflection on immersion events. Such elements particularly include the dignity of the human person, the common good, solidarity and subsidiarity. In recognising the presence of God in their experience, actions engaged in by those who have undergone transformation or conversion through immersion, are primarily actions seeking to influence others in some way. Regardless of whether these actions are immediate or longer-term, the process of theological reflection provides a pathway to transformation which is focused on God's mission.

Almost a year after the Philippines is when I started a conversation of, "There must be more to this", and that quest for 'the more' was solidified, and I started active pursuit of a volunteer placement program in Africa. The Philippines experience opened me up in that moment, in the eight days that we were there, and gave me the courage, I suppose, 12 months down the track, to do it on a grander scale. The rest is history. I stayed [teaching in a school in Africa] for 16 months.

(Ivy, Philippines)

Theological reflection invites people to view their experiences through a spiritual lens, thereby enabling them to actively participate in 'doing theology' rather than passively assimilating it. In offering a clearer understanding of the Christian tradition, people are better prepared to see the connection between it and their lived experience.

Engaging in theological reflection on events encountered on an immersion offers pathways to making meaning of the experience, and to discerning how the wisdom of the faith tradition might help to inform a spiritual response to that experience which engages the head, heart and hands.

Elements of Catholic Social Teaching help to inform a response to a theological reflection on immersion events...

CHAPTER 9
Soft eyes, warm heart

While immersions are generally found to be positive experiences for participants, the same cannot always be said for the people in the host community. 'Poverty tourism' which has come under scrutiny for its questionable ethical stance, and criticised as voyeurism, involves tourists visiting poverty-stricken areas in Majority World countries without interacting with local people. While the experience may be 'life-changing' for some participants, the outcomes for host communities have often been found to be less than favourable, as the visits have been criticised as highlighting the unequal encounter.

One of the most damaging criticisms is that short-term visitors go with preconceived notions of what is needed, encourage a 'hand-out' attitude in developing communities, and engage in activities that displace local labourers and professionals. Of even greater import is the potential for damage to fragile host communities. Student volunteer programs in particular are primarily concerned with broadening the mindsets of privileged young people who may have little or no experience outside their own locality.

An immersion group visited a Nicaraguan village and decided to purchase cows for the community…

> *When we go into these communities we must remember that we are visitors. We need to go with soft eyes and a warm heart.*
>
> Mary McDonald SGS

Concerns raised by both researchers and journalists have highlighted issues in which foreign interests have been prioritised over local ones, and in which critical reflection has failed to be encouraged in participants.

More recent developments have seen agencies such as ReThink Orphanages Australia and World Challenge advocating for an end to students volunteering in orphanages in countries such as Cambodia and Vietnam, due to exploitation of children and families.

Realistically, there are some participants who experience only a small, positive lasting change in their lives as a result of their immersion. Some return home disillusioned due to perceptions of inefficiency and corruption within the host country, and still others believe their presence may have had a negative impact on the host community.

The following reflections and activities provide different ways to consider the impact your immersion trip may have on the community you are visiting.

Think about, talk about...

Read through the following real-life situations and consider:
- How might these negative impacts have been mitigated?
- What opportunities do these insights offer?
- What challenges do they present?

1. An immersion group visited a Nicaraguan village and decided to purchase cows for the community. Later they learned that only one person there knew how to raise cows, and he lived outside of town. The cows all went to him, and the community project died.

2. A group of American high school students who had travelled to an orphanage in Tanzania to help build a library was so inept at laying bricks that each night the men in the village had to take down the structurally unsound bricks and re-lay them so that in the morning the students would be unaware of their failure.

3. A study found that it cost US$30,000 for volunteers to build a house in Honduras after Hurricane Mitch, while local Christian organisations built the same house for only US$2,000.

4. A church in Mexico was painted six times during one summer by six different immersion groups.

5. An Australian school changed their sports uniform and decided to donate the old style shirts, shorts and track suits to a community in India. This was done without dialogue with the community. The result was that a small sewing co-op that had been established by the local women through micro-finance was destroyed.

We come to bring Christ

To ancient hills,

To shrines and temples,

Among treasures left by artist and by poet

In scroll and in song.

Our round eyes are blind

To Christ in this land,

In this literature,

In this people.

We work, and await, expectantly, the beginnings of 'the Mission'

Slow learners, we find, at last, the heart of Mission –

Christ is here already,

Christ has been here always.

Christ, in Japan, still waits to be found.

Excerpt from First Impressions,
Rose Pekin SGS (written in 1978,
30 years after her arrival in Japan in 1948

The Monkeys and the Fish

The rainy season that year had been the strongest ever and the river had broken its banks. There were floods everywhere and the animals were all running up into the hills. The floods came so fast that many drowned except the lucky monkeys who used their proverbial agility to climb up into the treetops. They looked down on the surface of the water where the fish were swimming and gracefully jumping out of the water as if they were the only ones enjoying the devastating flood.

One of the monkeys saw the fish and shouted to his companion: "Look down, my friend, look at those poor creatures. They are going to drown. Do you see how they struggle in the water?" "Yes," said the other monkey. "What a pity! Probably they were late in escaping to the hills because they seem to have no legs. How can we save them?" "I think we must do something. Let's go close to the edge of the flood where the water is not deep enough to cover us, and we can help them to get out."

So the monkeys did just that. They started catching the fish, but not without difficulty. One by one, they brought them out of the water and put them carefully on the dry land. After a short time there was a pile of fish lying on the grass motionless. One of the monkeys said, "Do you see? They were tired, but now they are just sleeping and resting. Had it not been for us, my friend, all these poor people without legs would have drowned."

The other monkey said: "They were trying to escape from us because they could not understand our good intentions. But when they wake up they will be very grateful because we have brought them salvation."

Traditional Tanzanian Folktale

Think about, talk about...

1. What is the message of The Monkeys and the Fish for you?
2. How might this story influence your approach to planning an immersion trip?

CHAPTER 10

Conclusion

While gaining in popularity, short-term cross-cultural immersion is still an emerging phenomenon. In acknowledging the current Catholic landscape, in which connection of staff, students and parents to a worshipping community is limited, the provision of opportunities for personal engagement in action and advocacy offers distinctive access to another dimension of Catholic life, culture and mission.

The starting point for developing programs aimed at spiritual growth should be rooted in holistic concern for others, especially the disadvantaged and vulnerable. Designing immersion programs which intentionally situate participants in a cross-cultural setting in a Majority World community leads them to direct encounters with marginalised people. Engaging with the Gospel message through holistic concern for others in a meaningful context, opens the possibility for vocational motivation and capabilities for mission and service in the Church and the world.

In the current Australian Catholic educational landscape, the need for formation of all school community members is apparent, and a significant contribution can be made to this process by short-term cross-cultural immersion. The aims of formation for mission are well met by short-term cross-cultural immersion, and the growth of individuals and communities triggered by the experience is profound and ongoing.

In setting out to offer a guide for those wishing to undertake planning and facilitation of immersion trips within the Catholic context, this *Educator's Guide to Immersion* has drawn on the wisdom and experience of many who have walked with others in Majority World communities. Authentic encounters with God's people through immersion experiences provide unique opportunities for actively engaging in missionary discipleship. The transformative impact of re-placing oneself in the world and viewing the 'other' with soft eyes and a warm heart, enables new and visionary ways of living God's mission in the world today.

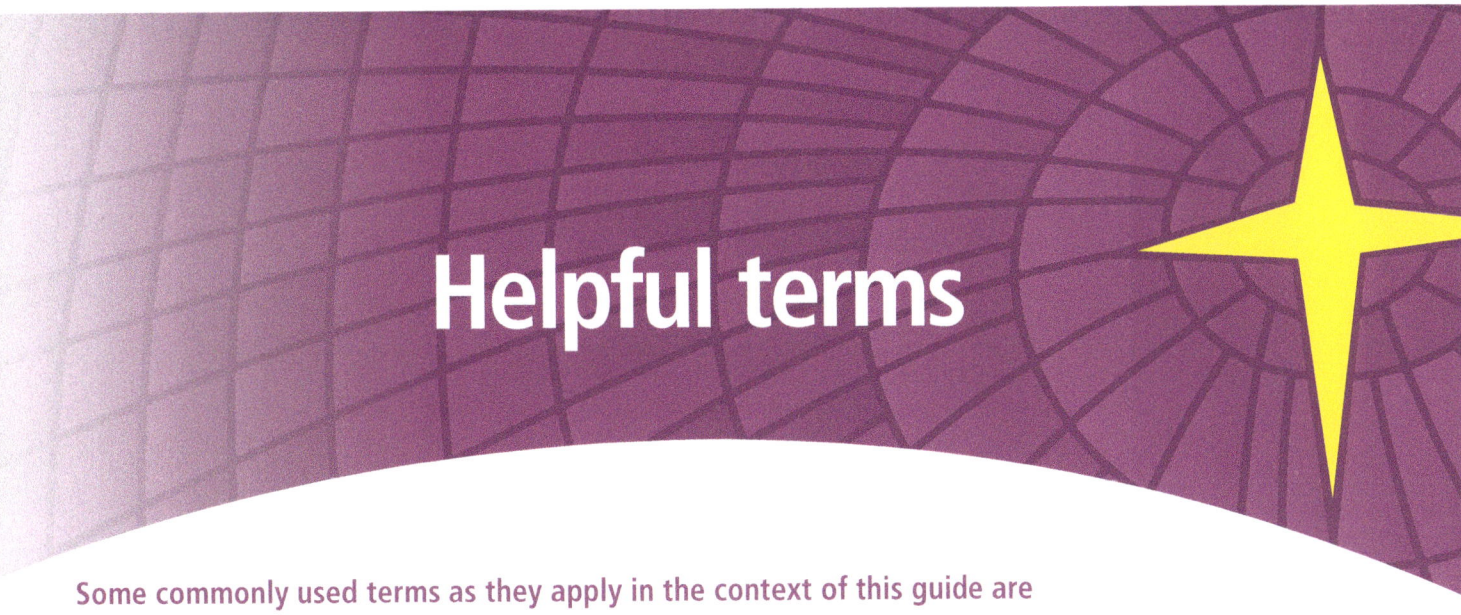

Helpful terms

Some commonly used terms as they apply in the context of this guide are defined and explained here.

CST
Catholic Social Teaching is a set of principles which offers a vision for a just society in which the dignity of all people is recognised and valued. Catholic Social Teaching provides guidance in regard to a vital element of the Church's mission in the world.

Charism
Drawing on the work of Maréchal, the understanding of charism[14] adopted for this guide is that it is:
A story to enter
A language to speak
A group to which to belong
A way to pray
A work to undertake
A face of God to see

Formation for Mission[2]
A contemporary understanding of formation of Catholic school community members is that it is 'Christ-centred'. It is an intentional, ongoing and reflective process that focuses on the growth of individuals and communities from their lived experiences, in spiritual awareness, theological understanding, vocational motivation and capabilities for mission and service in the Church and the world.

Host communities
Majority World communities which offer hospitality and partnership to visiting immersion groups.

Lectio Divina
This is 'divine reading', the traditional practice of slow, contemplative scriptural reading, meditation and prayer.

Majority World
This term refers to the regions of Asia, Africa, Latin America and Oceania, so-called as it comprises most of the world's population. Formerly referred to as the Third World or the Developing World[14], majority and minority worlds also exist in each society.

Mission
Mission is viewed by the community of believers as being for the reign of God in the world.[15] A contemporary approach is that it is not so much that God's Church has a mission, but rather, that God's mission has a Church.[16]

MPJP
A ministerial public juridic person is an entity under canon and civil law that allows the Church's ministries to function in the name of the Catholic Church.

Sending school
A school which selects participants for involvement in an immersion trip.

Short-term cross-cultural immersion
An experience during which participants visit and engage with local people in various settings in Majority World communities – usually for periods of less than two weeks.

Transformation
An internal change or shift experienced by an individual; changing a person from within.

Visio Divina
Drawing on the principles of Lectio Divina, Visio Divina (praying with the eyes) is the slow, thoughtful contemplation of a picture, photo, work of art, or any visual imagery.

Endnotes

1. Dutton, M (2015), *To be changed forever*. Retrieved from https://www.goodsams.org.au/article/to-be-changed-forever/.

2. D'Souza, S (2010), *Immersions: going anywhere?* Retrieved from http://www.edmundrice.net/ component/content/article/76-xriceexpress/555- immersions-going-anywhere.

3. Kearney, T (2010), *The impact of immersions*. Retrieved from http://www.edmundrice.net/component/ content/article/76-xriceexpress/608-immersions-a-impact.

4. National Catholic Education Commission (2017), *A framework for formation for mission in Catholic education*. Sydney, NSW National Catholic Education Commission.

5. Schroeder, R (2004), Entering someone else's garden: Cross-cultural mission/ministry. In Bevans, S B and Schroeder, R P, *Constants and context: A theology of mission for today*, Maryknoll, NY: Orbis Books.

6. Congregation for Catholic Education (2007), *Educating together in Catholic schools: A shared mission between consecrated persons and the lay faithful*, #46, Congregation for Catholic Education, Vatican City.

7. Gowdie, J D (2011), *Meaning and mission: Exploring a contemporary approach to spiritual formation for Catholic school educators*. PhD Thesis, Australian Catholic University, https://doi.org/10.4226/66/5a961094c6857

8. Brisbane Catholic Education, *Formation and leadership*. Retrieved from http:// www.bne.catholic.edu.au/religious-education-mission/Pages/Catching-Fire.aspx

9. Mezirow, J (1978), *Education for perspective transformation: Women's re-entry programs in community colleges*. Teacher's College, Columbia University, New York, NY.

10. Ross, S (2010), Transformative travel: An enjoyable way to foster radical change. *ReVision*, 31(1), 2010, pp. 54-61.

11. Trokan, J (1997), Models of Theological Reflection: Theory and Praxis, *Journal of Catholic Education*, 1 (2). http://dx.doi.org/10.15365/joce.0102041997

12. Whitehead, J & E (1995), *Method in Ministry: Theological Reflection and Christian Ministry*, Kansas City: Sheed & Ward.

13. Shea, J (1982), Storytelling and religious identity. *Chicago Studies*, Vol. 21 (I), pp. 23-43.

14. Maréchal, C (2002), *Toward an effective partnership between religious and laity in fulfilment of charism and responsibility for mission*. Paper presented at the 56th Conference of the Unione di Superiore Generale, Rome.

15. Phan, P C (2002), *The gift of the Church: A textbook on ecclesiology*, Collegeville, MN: The Liturgical Press.

16. Bevans, S (2009), *The mission has a church: An invitation to the dance*. Melbourne, VIC: Yarra Theological Union.

Suggested further reading

Beyerlein, K., Trinitapoli, J., & Adler, G. (2011). The effect of religious short-term mission trips on youth civic engagement. *Journal for the Scientific Study of Religion*, 50(4), 780-795.

Coghlan, A., & Gooch, M. (2011). Applying a transformative learning framework to volunteer tourism. *Journal of Sustainable Tourism*, 19(6), 713-728.

Connolly, N. (2016). *A great welcome for ourselves.* Retrieved from: https://www.columban.org. au/media-and-publications/newsletters-and-bulletins/columban-ebulletin/archive/2016/ e-news-vol.9-no.6/fr-noel-connolly-a-great-welcome-for-ourselves

Curry-Stevens, A. (2007). New forms of transformative education: Pedagogy for the privileged. *Journal of Transformative Education*, 5(1), 33-58.

Donaldson, A. (2010). *Encountering God in the margins: reflections of a justice volunteer*. Ireland: Veritas.

Dutton, M. (2019). *The contribution of short-term cross-cultural immersion to the formation of Catholic school staff*. Doctoral Thesis, Australian Catholic University, https://doi.org/10.26199/5ddf4c031bd87.

Fanning, D. (2009). Short Term Missions: A trend that is growing exponentially. *Trends and Issues in Missions*, 4, 1-31.

Johnson, L. A. (2014). Can short-term mission trips reduce prejudice? *The Journal for the Sociological Integration of Religion and Society*, 4(1), 10-22.

Jones, S. R., Rowan-Kenyon, H. T., Ireland, S. M., Niehaus, E., & Skendall, K. C. (2012). The meaning students make as participants in short-term immersion programs. *Journal of College Student Development*, 53(2), 201-220.

Palacios, C. M. (2010). Volunteer tourism, development and education in a postcolonial world: Conceiving global connections beyond aid. *Journal of Sustainable Tourism*, 18(7), 861-878.

Plante, T., Lackey, K., & Hwang, J. (2009). The impact of immersion trips on development of compassion among college students. *Journal of Experiential Education*, 32, 28-43.

Probasco, L. (2013). Giving time, not money: Long-term impacts of short-term mission trips. *Missiology: An International Review*, 4(2), 202-224.

Woloshyn, V. E., & Grierson, A. L. (2015). Secondary-school students' international voluntourism experiences: Effects on worldviews, behaviours and aspirations. *Journal of the International Society for Teacher Education*, 19(1), 48-59.

Wright, S., & Hodge, P. (2012). To be transformed: Emotions in cross-cultural, field-based learning in Northern Australia. *Journal of Geography in Higher Education*, 36(3), 355-368.

List of Figures

Figure 1 Guiding principles for immersion for mission

Figure 2 Three phases of the immersion process

Figure 3 Reflection process before planning an immersion

Figure 4 Perspectives for consideration in planning an immersion

Figure 5 Helpful perspectives in planning an immersion

Figure 6 Reflection template for immersion planning

Figure 7 Trokan's Praxis of Theological Reflection

Acknowledgments

My doctoral research was the impetus for this project, and I am forever grateful for the support and direction of my supervisory team. I would like to acknowledge, with gratitude and thanks, my Principal Supervisors Dr Roger Vallance FMS and Dr Joseph Zajda, whose expertise, guidance and professionalism were very much appreciated. Also, my Assistant Supervisor, Dr Wendy Moran. Her enthusiasm, encouragement, and meticulous attention to detail were always highly motivating and gratefully received.

The dedication and commitment of the Sisters of the Good Samaritan – particularly in the communities of the Philippines, Kiribati, Timor-Leste, Japan and indigenous communities in Australia – have been the inspiration for this guide. I would like to thank each and every one them, and especially the people living in these communities – their hospitality and generosity of spirit know no bounds.

I would like to thank my former colleagues in Good Samaritan Education – the Governing Council, Assembly, principals, and all the wonderful staff members who so generously shared their experiences of immersion. The depth, honesty and intensity of their reflections are profoundly moving and deeply appreciated.

I would like to thank in particular, Dr Mary McDonald SGS. Her wisdom and vision were the impetus for the Staff Immersion Program which was the basis for my research, and for this guide. I am extremely grateful for her mentorship, friendship, support and advice over many years.

I am indebted also to Sr Rita Hayes SGS. My first immersion experience was in the tiny mountain hamlets of Timor-Leste where Rita was working in the school and the community. The impact of her inspirational work continues and the scholarship program she began has enabled young people and communities to thrive and flourish.

I would also like to thank Sr Meg Kahler SGS, who shared so many of the immersion journeys which feature in this guide. Her innate understanding of the human condition and the importance of intercultural relationships have been a source of inspiration and constant learning for me. I am humbled by her giftedness. Her ongoing belief and encouragement in my research and this guide are sincerely appreciated.

Special thanks go to Jim and Therese D'Orsa. Their contribution to mission and education in the Australian Catholic landscape is profoundly inspiring, and a source of wisdom and vision for all who seek to build kingdom spaces in their life, work, mission and ministry. Thank you for your faith in the significance of this work and your belief in the importance of this guide.

Thanks also to Karen Tayleur and her wonderful team at Garratt Publishing. Their creativity in the layout and design work have brought the text to life.

Finally, I would like to dedicate this guide to my family. To my husband Mark; to Michael, Sarah, Jack and Ivy; to Nikki, Heath and Madison; and to Chris. Your never-ending love and support bring meaning and joy to my life, beyond your imagining. Thank you!

www.ingramcontent.com/pod-product-compliance
Lightning Source LLC
Chambersburg PA
CBHW040316240426
43663CB00025B/2978